LET MEDITATION HAPPEN

By

SWAMI ANUBHAVANANDA SARASWATI

मौज में रहो

Be Happy Inc. USA
Yo Veda Inc. Australia
Sat Bhavana Trust, India
Happy Folks of South Africa

Indra Publishing House
www.indrapublishing.com

Published by:

Indra Publishing House
E-5/21, Arera Colony,
Habibganj Police Station Road,
Bhopal- 462016
Phone : +91 755-4059620, 4030921
Telefax : +91 755-4030921
Email : manish@indrapublishing.com
        pramod@indrapublishing.com
Web. : www.indrapublishing.com

© Sat Bhavana Trust, India
Be Happy Inc. USA
Yo Veda Inc. Australia
Happy Folks of South Africa
www.justbehappy.org

First Print 2010
Second Print : 2014
ISBN : 978-81-89107-74-1
₹ : 250/-

Printed & published by Mr. Manish Gupta for Indra Publishing House, E-5/21, Arera Colony, Habibganj Police Station Road, Bhopal- 462016 INDIA

All rights reserved. No part of this publication may be reproduced, stored in or introduced into a retrieval system, or transmitted, in any form or by any means without the prior written permission of the author. Any person who does any unauthorized act in relation to this publication may be liable to criminal prosecution and civil claims for damages.

Information contained in this work is obtained by the publishers from sources believed to be reliable. The publisher and its authors make no representation or warranties with respect to accuracy or completeness of the contents of this book and shall not be liable for any errors, omission or damages arising out of use of this information. Dispute if any related to this publication is subject to Bhopal Jurisdiction.

अभिप्रायः।

श्रीमस्तु स्वामिपादपद्मसु

सप्रश्रयं साष्टाङ्गप्रणामाः।

'अद्वितीं कार्यम् । अत्र वेदान्त सांख्य-योग प्रभृति दर्शनानां न केवलं समावेशः अपितु तेषां रहस्योद्घाटनपरा व्याख्यापि असामान्यत्वं लभते।' अत्र भवतां- 'आर्षदृष्टिः'-अपरोक्षानुभूतिसंवलिता वैचारिकी वा विशेषेण विभाविता वर्तते। सुधीभिरघ्यात्मजिज्ञासापरैरध्यानगन्तृभि - श्च असंशयं स्वानुरूपो लाभो भावयितव्यः:- इति मेऽभिप्सा। कृष्णवैर्णैः यत्किञ्चिदल्पधिया मया समीक्षितं तद्भवद्भिः करूणापरैः समालोच्य, तथा च यत्र तत्र यल्लिखितं तद् विचारीयत्वं गमिष्यति-इत्येषा च सविनयं प्रार्थ्यतं।'

भवतां विधेयः
आचार्यो राम रत्न शास्त्री

Introduction

The meditation sessions mentioned in this book were conducted for the Vedanta students at Kaivalyadham, Lonavala, during the year 2007. All sessions were recorded for those who wanted a help in practicing them subsequent to the course. The technical authenticity was verified and substantiated by Shri.Ram Ratna Shastri, a scholar from Kaivalyadham. His views are attached in the Foreword of the present publication in original Sanskrit. His sincerity and efforts are much more than a mere reference and appreciation.

These sessions were conducted primarily for Vedanta students who were also exhaustively exposed to Patanjal Yoga Darshan. This was a rare combination for both the students of Yoga as well as students of Vedanta.

Mere Vedantic talk without Yogic practices leads to an argumentative personality, ever ready to condemn and belittle other branches of spiritual scriptures. Similarly, yogic practices without the correct understanding of 'Jiva', 'Jagat' and 'Ishwara' (as relative expressions of the absolute Reality existing in mutual dependence), becomes merely a physical, health oriented approach or a means for developing some occult powers.

The present sessions of meditations have a balanced weightage given to both sciences to ultimately discover the absolute Reality which is simultaneously transcendental to and immanent in the relativity.

The tedious and time consuming job of listening, transcribing, editing and giving it a book form was enthusiastically undertaken by Mrs. Seema Agarwal of Ahmedabad, who deserves all the credit in bringing it out in the present print.

We pray to the Almighty, 'May the seekers of Truth merge in the Divine Glory and be a source of light to one and all.'

Swami Anubhavananda
1.1.2009

FIRST READ THIS!!!

Please start reading the book from the first page.
The scheme of thought is as under.

1. The first few talks are lengthy and exhaustive, giving a complete picture of why, how, when, where, whose, in meditation.
2. The goal and the non achievement in meditation.
3. The cautions and pitfalls on account of earlier default settings.
4. Do's and don'ts spread throughout the instructions.
5. Beware you won't get anything but you'll get lost and what can not be lost is the real you from whom the virtual you has been highlight-shift-deleted!

Meditations start from:
1. Body
2. Thoughts
3. Chanting
4. Pranayama
5. Mr. Nobody!

MEDITATION 1

In any meditational session that you have done in the past, you most probably kept matter as the primary factor in your meditation. This means that you remain objective.

What are the experiences that you have gone through?

Either you were not able to sit properly.

If you were able to sit properly, then the breathing was not proper.

If the breathing was proper, then the mind was disturbed.

If the mind was not disturbed, then you started imagining various kinds of things!

In all this, what is happening is, we are remaining objective and the objective phenomena is the most primary for us.

So, like we see the world around us, on the seat of meditation, too, we continue to be objective.

When we continue to be objective, the duality, I versus you, 'atma versus anatma', self versus not self, this continues as an underlying note throughout life.

The Upanishad says, 'As long as there is someone or something other, three things cannot be removed from our system.

They are, Desire, Anger and Fear.

So, the load of desire, anger and fear will continue to bother us throughout our lives, whatever meditation we may do, this relativity or duality is kept intact and disturbs us.

Therefore, the first thing that we have to do, is that we have to be very systematically and clearly subjective in our approach.

Not objective. Now, the second and most important thing is that, we must have a clear destination and a clear road map.

If you are going and there is no clarity of goal, then what happens is, we drag ourselves, here and there.

If you see taxi drivers, when they have a customer sitting in the car, the destination is clear, they know the road well, therefore they go very fast.

But, when there is no customer sitting, then they don't know where to go.

So, when the destination is not there, the path also is not known.

The destination also determines the path.

So, when we are sitting for meditation, are we sitting for doing meditation, for the sake of doing meditation?

We eat food. Are we eating food just for the sake of eating food?

No. There is some purpose, some goal. In the same manner, many of us are struggling, wanting to do meditation.

We need to remove all the wrong notions that we have about meditation, in our mind. Firstly, meditation is not a verb.

A verb is that which initiates action.

Like, 'I am going'. So, to go is a verb. Similarly, 'I am meditating'.

So, meditation has become a verb. Whenever there is an action, there is a doer. Therefore, when 'I am going', I is there. And when 'I am meditating', I is there.

So, whether I am doing something or I am doing meditation, This 'I', the culprit behind all the problems, is kept intact.

And then, in any activity in the world, when some action is successful, 'I' is very happy. When some action is not successful, 'I' is very miserable. The same thing happens in meditation.

'Oh, today the meditation was really good! I have done such a beautiful meditation.'

And the next day, 'I don't know what happened today. Yesterday the meditation was really good. Today it did not happen properly. I did not do it well. I don't know where I went wrong!'

So, the 'I' is only changing the uniform.

Earlier the 'I' had the uniform that 'I am happy'. Now, the same 'I' has the uniform that 'I am miserable'.

Earlier I had the uniform that I am an extrovert and hence, a worldly person.

Now, I has put on another uniform, that I am an introvert and spiritual person.['I' is being used as a third person singular pronoun]

Thus the 'samsara' continues.

Let Meditation Happen

So, the first thing that we have to clearly bring in our understanding, is that meditation is not an action.

One day, a lady asked me, 'Swamiji, can you teach me to do meditation?'

I said, 'Yes', and then asked her more about herself. She said that she was the mother of two children, aged seven and nine.

"Do you love them?" I asked.

"Of course" came her quick reply!

"Can you tell me how you love them?"

She couldn't reply to that.

"When you carried the first child in your womb, your mother-in-law and mother must have given you lots of instructions. Don't do this, don't eat this food, don't go there, don't lift heavy things, don't read bad books, don't be moody.....etc..

Similarly, when the baby was born, they must have once again given lots of instructions. Feed the baby properly, change the nappies regularly. But did any of them tell you, that you have to love your child? And when you started loving your child, did you ask your mother, 'Mom, please tell me how you loved me, so that I can love my child in the same manner? No."

Now, let us go into the depth of the matter, and not see things from the surface level. That will never help us. The mother or the father, they love their child only for one reason.

The reason is, the mother or the father, find themselves extended in another body. So, as much as I love myself, I love my own child.

Because, this I is no more limited in this body, but, the I is now extended in another body.

Otherwise, this child who has newly arrived in the world, we don't know anything about him, yet we start loving him. That means, that we can love even an unknown child.

So, what is the reason for this love?

We find ourselves reflected in the child, and that is the only reason that we love the child.

A long time back, in a hospital, one of my friends' wife was admitted for delivery. The nurse, due to some exchange of hot words, was very angry with my friend and would not allow him to see his wife. He called me, 'Swamiji, what should I do?'

So, I went there. It was my first visit ever to a maternity ward. The nurse allowed me in but not the husband. The babies all had a tag attached to them with their room numbers. So, when I went in to meet the mother, the nurse brought the baby in. 'Oh, how sweet, how cute!', The mother exclaimed. I asked them to check the tag properly and it so turned out that she had brought in another baby. "Oh, Swamiji, you are right! This is not the one!"

Now, see, that child which was unknown, but when you were told that it is your baby, immediately love started flowing. But, when you were told that, That was not your child, but the other baby was yours, that moment your love changed immediately. How do you do that?

Friends, please understand one basic thing. Don't struggle on the seat of meditation.

Let it happen. It is something like, how the fruit matures or ripens on the tree, and detaches effortlessly, that fruit has got a great fragrance, great taste.

In the same manner, let our meditation happen.

When the fruit ripens, it detaches from the tree without any effort.

In the same manner,

Until our understanding about ourselves, Our understanding about the world, Our understanding about God, Our understanding about mutual relationships, Becomes clear and distinct, we will only be struggling. We read various books by various authors.

Each author uses words to mean something different from other authors.

Like, 'consciousness, awareness', then we only keep groping in darkness. Consciousness is the reality.

'What is the meaning of consciousness?'

'No, you cannot talk about consciousness. Consciousness is the reality.'

Let Meditation Happen

So, I will have my imagination of consciousness.
You will have your imagination of consciousness.
The third person will have a third imagination of consciousness.
Thus, there will always be something different.
Never meaning the same truth.
Therefore, we will be trying to understand, what is the authority on the basis of which we will be practicing meditation,
Or, we will be attaining culmination of our life in meditation.
Meditation happens only once. Once it happens, it never reverts back. Just like every age you have gone through. Childhood, teenage, middle age. They all come only once.
In the same manner, there is no reverting back in meditation.
There is no repetition in meditation.
Repetition is possible only in the finite.
In infinity, repetition is not possible.
As infinity is one without a second.
Therefore, all our meditation will be based upon the foundation of understanding. Not on the foundation of mechanical struggle or acrobatics. Like, even if you sit in a particular posture, that is secondary. Primary is understanding. And when understanding is clear, we will come to know, that when we had been struggling on the seat of meditation, it was uncalled for. It was not required.
So, meditation starts happening with the maturity and clarity of understanding. Now, meditation is not a regular drill for a short period of time. One hour meditation and rest of the twenty three hours frustration.
Then that meditation will be frustrated meditation. That is not meditation. There is something called as cause and effect. We are all caught up in this. The mind cannot function without cause and effect. When we get caught up in this cause and effect, We go away from our own selves. So, one must have clarity of goal in one's life. We have to live a purposeful life and not a mechanical life. Whenever life becomes mechanical, it loses it's charm.
We get up in the morning, read the paper, have breakfast, all in

Let Meditation Happen

a very routine manner. One gets bored.

The same thing happens with those who walk the spiritual path.

They also get bored if they become mechanical in their spiritual pursuit. Then I get these kind of questions, 'Swamiji, earlier I was an extremely spiritual person, but these days I don't know what has happened. I don't feel like getting up in the morning, I don't feel like chanting the Lord's name.'

One middle aged lady, asked me this question,

"Swamiji, when I got married, my husband was 25, and I was 22. I was very interested in worldly things.

Going for vacations, cinema, movies, enjoying everything.

But, he was extremely spiritual and I used to get fed up with him.

He would take me for satsang and soon I got involved in all that.

Now, our son has completed graduation and may get married anytime. So, because of so many years of satsang, I now spend more of my time in studies and contemplation. And my husband has become the other way round.

Now he wants to go for drama, movies and here and there.

I am no more interested in all this.

I don't know what is happening."

So, when she was not interested in the spiritual path, he was.

Now, she is into it and he is not.

In this manner, life becomes very messy.

So, she asked me what she should do.

I told her, "See, God has planned this particular situation for you.

Earlier you had this impression that only when you sit on the seat of meditation, you are in meditation.

When you offered food to the lord, it was your devotion.

This has got you to a particular level.

Now extend that in every activity of your life.

So even if you go for a movie with your husband, that should not disturb you. That is your next step in 'sadhana'". If this is not understood, then we get lost. Now my path is different, your path is different. You go this way, I go that way.

Let Meditation Happen

This is not the way! Therefore, meditation is not a drill to be done at a particular time of a day. For a short or long period of time. No. It is living in understanding, awareness, consciousness. Then the next step. The mind is caught up in cause and effect. Out of these two options, when the mind is caught up at the level of effect, The mind will continue to be disturbed. There are two words in Sanskrit. 'Abhivyakti' and 'vyakti', Meaning 'manifestation' and 'manifested entity' respectively. 'Abhivyakti' is at the level of cause and 'vyakti' is at the level of effect.

Ornaments are manifestations of gold at the level of cause. This ornament is mine is at the level of effect. Manifestation is a generalized principle and a particular manifestation by which we get totally bound and caught up in, is the individuality. Take a few examples to understand. Then you will come to the conclusion that meditation is the journey from the 'vyakti' to the 'abhivyakti'. From individuality to manifestation.

One day a very disturbed lady came to me.

"Swamiji, where will we go when our husbands don't listen to us? My in-laws are terrible, and that is why I have come to you. My son wants to get married to a girl who is not good looking."

Now, take this as the beginning of understanding. A boy getting married to any girl. This is a general principle happening anywhere in the world. Now, when we hear about it, what happens to us? We become philosophical. "Nowadays, boys are also going like that and girls are also going like that. What can we do? It is OK. Accept it."

But, when the same thing happens to 'My son. My son getting married to someone I don't like!!'

So, a son getting married to a girl you don't like or a good looking girl, Whatever it is, this is a general phenomena happening all over the world. It does not create a problem. But, the problem is created when we associate it with the manifestation at a limited level. If this is understood, then apply this principle. There is pain in the body. Naturally, pain happens in the body. Body is an abode of pain. It is OK.

Let Meditation Happen

But, when the pain happens to me. Then it is a big issue! Therefore, our identification with the finite, is the cause of miseries in our life. Effect is finite. Cause is infinite. So, what is meditation? It is giving up our hold on the finite and growing slowly into the infinite. When we come at the level of infinite, the problems of finite disappear. Now, take an example to understand this. We are all miserable, disturbed, angry etc.. When? When we become somebody in life. As a mother, father, sister, teacher, student. As a warden, cook, master, Whenever we have become somebody. That becoming somebody is getting identified with a finite role. So, we get identified with so many finite roles. Every identification with each finite role gives us its own quota of miseries.

So, what is the sum total of all these finite roles?

That we are infinitely miserable.

Then such people have nothing but complaints.

'My wife is like that, children are like that'.

Anywhere they go, they cannot see the beauty in this world.

Because they have trained themselves to get lost in the finite and become miserable. Such a person who has been living at the level of finite existence, gets tired, exhausted, miserable, Because of the load of the small finites that he carries on his head. Friends, what finally happens to such a person, is that, he wants to drop everything. And to drop everything, we have only one option. That is, to go to sleep. When we enter sleep, We drop identification with the small finite things. Then we are neither mother, sister, child, Indian,

All the small things which we carry on our head, We drop in our deep sleep experience and we come to the level of the cause.

So, when our experience is at the cause level,

There is bliss. When we start living at the effect level,

There are blisters. There is misery.

If this is sincerely clear in our understanding,

What will be the meditation?

Meditation will be the abidance at the level of the cause and not as an effect.

Let Meditation Happen

Now all those people who are miserable on account of small things, What they have to do is, They have to rise above these small things. We are all miserable for something or the other. Now find out.

Are any of us miserable because we could not be in the position of the President of America?

Is anyone miserable because of that?

No.

This thought never even enters our mind!

We get miserable about, 'Today I did not get hot water for my bath.' So, from a small little thing we become awfully miserable.

Small things are many. Big things are few. Mosquitoes are many. Elephants are few. Similarly, wise people are few. Ignorant are many. In the same manner, the infinite reality is one. The finite, individuality are many.

So, meditation is giving up our position as an effect, an individual, and merge in the cause. For the wave, which is an effect,

There is always competition, struggle, birth, growth, fighting, decay, old age and death.

This is the story of a wave.

What is the story of the ocean?

No birth, no competition, no decay, no death.

So, when one wave sees another wave dying, If it is an enemy, 'Good'. If it is a near and dear one, 'Oh, I am very miserable.' What will be the experience of the ocean, When it is constantly seeing the births and deaths of millions of waves?

He knows that all of them are born in me, remain in me and come back to me.

When we go to the level of the cause, The birth and the death of the effect is equal. When more and more waves are erupting on the surface of the ocean, The ocean does not become rich.

When the waves are quiet and there is barely a ripple on the surface of the ocean, The ocean has not become poor. When gold is living as an ornament,

Let Meditation Happen

You can remove or add something to make it small or big. But, you add more ornaments in the gold, the gold does not change.

If you dissolve the ornaments and make it a lump of gold, nothing is lost. Therefore, what will meditation be?

It will be that we have to live consciously as the cause and not as an effect. When we start living as the cause,

The cause has more understanding. Effect will never understand that both the waves are expressions of the same ocean. One wave will never understand the other wave. If you have two-three children, you must have experienced. During childhood, they fight with each other for every small little thing.

But, what is the understanding of the parents?

They know that it is OK.

But, when the same children are grown up, strong, and don't listen to their parents, Parents say, 'You don't understand what I am telling you, but when you become a parent, you will understand.' When the child becomes a parent, they say, 'Mom, you were right. I did not listen to you.' But, it doesn't matter. This is carried on from generation to generation. So, meditation is giving up the position of effect and coming to the position of cause. When there is misery, it can be attributed to somebody or something.

Misery has come because of the neighbor, husband, children....

But, to become miserable or not, That is an option given to us by the Lord! So, if we are miserable in this world, it is our own choice. When we have chosen to be miserable, who can help us? Nobody can help. Therefore, what will be the meditation, now. Meditation will be the inquiry into, Who is doing the meditation. Of course, I am doing it. So, I as a father is miserable, I as a son is miserable. I as a student is miserable. So, if there is no 'I',

If 'I' the husband dies, can I say what will happen to 'my' wife?

No. Because 'I' is the foundation of 'my'. If there is no 'I' there is no 'My'.

What does living at the level of cause mean?

Living at the level of cause is living at the level of this 'I'.

Let Meditation Happen

When this 'I' is identified with the gross body, he is Mr. waker and the gross world becomes real. When the same 'I' is identified with the modifications of the mind only, and not the gross body, then this 'I' becomes the dreamer and the dream world of thoughts alone becomes the reality. And when this 'I' gets identified with the absence of waking and dream experience, The same 'I' becomes the deep sleeper. So, this I is not worthy of trusting. Sometimes he is a waker, dreamer or deep sleeper. So why don't we find out who the real 'I' is. We are now coming out of the effect level and going into the cause level.

As to who is miserable?
Who is suffering?
Who is enjoying?
This is how meditation is a conscious effort, wherein,
We drop the objective lifestyle.

The objective lifestyle is that lifestyle, which takes us away from ourselves. We are of the nature of bliss.

Otherwise, why do we seek bliss?
We are not of the nature of misery.
Or else, why would we want to get rid of misery?
Like sugar is never tired of carrying sweetness.
Fire is never tired of carrying heat.

In the same manner, we become tired of carrying misery because it is not our nature. We are all seeking bliss because that is our nature.

So, we are essentially, basically of the nature of bliss.

If you are standing in light, and you go away from light, means what?

You go in darkness. Going away from light is going towards darkness. Similarly, we are essentially of the nature of bliss. So, going away from one's self, Will be going towards misery. So, whenever we are miserable, We have strayed away from our own essential self. Now understand the cause and effect. Cause is infinite blissful existence. Effect is finite, miserable, temporary existence. We can be blissful all the time.

Let Meditation Happen

We cannot be miserable all the time. Therefore, meditation is going from the finite into the infinite. Say there is a pot. Outside there is space. Now, the pot also has space. We will call it pot space. Pot space is finite. Because it is finite, if you put something foul smelling into it, it will smell foul. If you put in something good smelling, it will smell good. Because of the space containing good or bad contents. Now, if the pot space has to merge in the total space,

Where will the pot have to go?

Nowhere. Because total space is available everywhere. The pot doesn't have to go anywhere. Does the pot require breaking the walls? No. There is no need.

Only give zero importance to the walls, because of which the total space is called pot space. Pot space is essentially total space, But, what happens is, Because of the importance and utilitarian approach, Pot space is useful for taking a cup of tea. In the total space, you cannot drink a cup of tea. Therefore, slowly we start taking the finite as real. And when we take the finite as real, Then our realization also becomes real. As if we are not realized now.

Whether we want or we don't want, we are essentially conscious blissful existence. But if I don't want to be? I am sorry, you are.

Where is the problem?

The problem is in non recognition of our own essential nature. This is the basic difference between matter oriented meditation and understanding oriented meditation. In case of matter oriented meditation, we will only be paying more and more attention to the paraphernalia. We should have this kind of mattress. Like the gun of the terrorist, students carry this big mattress. That becomes a major thing with us. We have to discover the absolute reality. The most important principle to be learnt and digested by every seeker, is that, in the relative world, There is zero possibility of absolute happiness. In the relative world, we do get happiness, But, it is relative happiness. You carry two bags in your hands. One heavy and one light and you have to go climbing up to a temple. One hand which is carrying a heavy bag, and one hand which is carrying a light bag. After some time, you put the heavy bag down and it feels very good. So, that goodness is only relative. Then after some time we change the bags in each hand. Similarly, in our lives, we have only recognized relative happiness. First of all I get married to get happiness. Then I discover that I am miserable. Then I seek divorce.

Am I happy after the divorce?

No. I am lonely. So, I get married again and the same cycle continues. In this manner, we go from one relativity to another, but, never reach the absolute!

Therefore, meditation is getting out of the catch of relative experiences. And arriving at the absolute experience. Where the experiencer and the experienced division disappears. When there is an experience without the experiencer, it is the absolute. When it is knowledge without the knower, it is absolute. When it is joy without an enjoyer, it is absolute. Having discovered this absolute reality to be our essential being, thereafter we don't have to be afraid. Otherwise, we are afraid that the thoughts will come. Don't look that side, or the thoughts will come.

Are we afraid of thoughts or what??

Life is not a fearful existence. We have to discover the truth only once. Not many times. Like you have to know swimming only once. We don't have to learn it again and again. If you want to get a medal, then you have to struggle.

But, as regards the principle of swimming is concerned, we learn it only once and thereafter, even if we want, we cannot forget it. We cannot drown if we know swimming. The same thing is true in case of recognition of the infinite self. But, if you are holding on only at the level of matter, and you practice for a long period of time, sitting in a particular posture. But, then you give up your practice. Don't sit. Within the period of few days or months, once your practice is gone, you start getting pain here and there, because in prakruti, in matter, in the finite alone, practice is valid. In infinite, there is no practice possible. Because practice means, repeating the same thing.

Let Meditation Happen

Words can be repeated. Silence cannot. Words are created. Silence is not. And with more and more understanding and awareness, when we start living our lives 24 hours, then every moment we are practicing meditation. Otherwise, like we look at the world, we start looking at our experiences. We have to have a clear understanding and with this clarity of understanding, we will know that meditation is nothing but 'paramatma', absolute reality. It is the uncreated experience of conscious blissful existence. It is not created because of anything. Anything created will be destroyed. Anything created will have a beginning and an end. Anything created cannot be perfect.

The uncreated alone is perfect. Meditation is not the effect of effort. It is being ourselves. It is not becoming somebody. Therefore, let us understand meditation. Whenever anything is a result of understanding, it has a lasting effect. If it happens just by fluke, it cannot last long. Suppose you take a gun, and shoot, And you hit the target by fluke. You will not be sure to hit it a second time because you don't know how it happened the first time.

In the same manner, when we grow in understanding about ourselves, we grow in understanding about the world, we grow in understanding about God, we grow in understanding about relationships. Then meditation starts happening. Our life goes smoothly like flowing water. Without effort. Thereafter life is lived. There is no 'body' who is struggling through life.

✦✦✦

MEDITATION 2

Most of you must have attended 'satsang'. But that must have been according to your own convenience. Amidst your worldly activities, you must have squeezed in some time for meditation, studies or 'satsang', whenever you felt the need for it.

This is how you have been shuttling between the world at one end and 'satsang' at the other end. Whenever we live such a life, there is zero self discipline. Without self discipline we cannot achieve anything in our lives. Whatever we want to do, whenever we want to do, wherever we want to go, whatever is convenient to us, that is not freedom. That is slavery to the mind.

Therefore, while we will be reading and then doing these meditations, we will implement total self discipline. Were you thinking that spiritual life is simple? No. It is not simple and self discipline may be difficult and you will find it tough. The only reason being that you will lose your wrong freedom.

Bhagwan Shri Krishna has said, 'Those who are completely, fully devoted to me and living in me all the time, everywhere, in every situation, I take care of their requirements and protection.' Isn't it beautiful. But, as regards the experience of this is concerned, we lack it.

This is because our understanding of spiritual life is like one of our many pursuits. Drawing, music, gardening, like these things. We do it to kill time. Otherwise the mind will kill us. That is the only reason. We practice the spiritual 'sadhanas', according to our own convenience. This is how we are unable to be aware of the fact, that the mind is ruling us.

Therefore, self discipline is really important. If self discipline is not attained, then you will struggle throughout your life, on the seat of meditation, and will only be frustrated.

That is why, listening to Vedanta or talking about Vedanta is not the end. Katha Upanishad very clearly states, 'Only by delivering lectures or listening to lectures the truth is not revealed. Only by remembering the text, verses, word by word, the truth is not revealed. He who has chosen the truth and the truth alone, to the exclusion of everything else in the world, to him alone the truth is revealed.'

Does that mean that we all have to take 'sanyas'? No. Please don't do that and compete with me! That is not the meaning. The meaning is, when we remain self disciplined the mind listens to us. Self discipline at the level of the body is the method to control the mind, which is whipping the body from behind.

When the mind becomes disciplined, then you sit on the seat of meditation, you will have zero disturbance. At this moment what happens to us is, that the more we want to sit quietly, the more the mind becomes turbulent. The reason being, we have not taken care of this aspect of the mind.

Doing whatever you feel like doing, that is not freedom. This is the American method of freedom. I want to take a gun and go shoot the children in a school. There, you are a citizen of a free country. That is not freedom.

There are three 'I's.

Information

Interaction

Implementation

You are being given the information.

Interaction is the awareness of every moment that we practice meditation. Are we leaving the old style? Are we insisting on whatever we have decided? The mind plays certain tricks on us. We see only what we have already decided to see. We don't see what is. First we decide, and then we see that everywhere. There was this man who was sitting in the first class compartment in a train. Probably for the first time in his life. The train stopped and a poor villager got in. 'Is this train going to Delhi?', he asked the man. Now, the normal reply would have been, a simple 'yes' or 'no'. But, the reply given by the man was, 'No. No. This is first class. Go away!' I was just sitting there and observing. I had nothing to talk. This is how I

Let Meditation Happen

learn in my life. That man had already conditioned his mind, that I am sitting in the first class and how can this poor fellow come and sit in the first class?

Such a thing happens when our interactions with our perceptions are biased. Working on the mind is the most subtle operation in the whole universe. We may control the oceans, we may control the winds, we may control the world, but, controlling one's mind is a real great achievement. Self discipline is required for that.

Self discipline is followed under two conditions.

One, the discipline is accepted as a burden from outside. Whenever this happens, we suffer in a disciplined manner. So we are disciplined also and we suffer also. Such people are the majority in the whole world.

The second type of people are those, who accept self discipline by their own choice. So, when discipline is accepted willingly, there is no burden of discipline.

When a sculptor goes in search of a stone for making a beautiful idol, he searches everywhere. After he has selected the stone, he has already planned out a particular picture in his mind of the statue that he is going to carve out.

Then he makes the lines on the stone, as he had imagined in his mind. He checks it from all the sides. He decides what has to be removed, rubbed, kept, filled, chiseled etc..

After all this is done, he is ready with the chisel and hammer and he starts. In the same manner, before we plunge deep into meditation, these preparations are extremely necessary.

Yoga is the most misused word in the whole world, today. Suddenly we want to do meditation, Samadhi. Patanjali Yoga Darshan describes the eight steps in Yoga.

Yama Niyama Asana Pranayama Pratyahara Dharana Dhyana And Samadhi.

Only after these are we qualified for deep meditation. But, we take the initial steps for granted and that is the reason that we are not able to find any fulfillment in spite of sincere efforts. There is sincerity but there is no wisdom applied to the sincerity. That is why we have to go step by step. In a meditation camp, we don't have time to go through these initial stages and we go straight into meditation. But, here we are not in a hurry. You must have prepared eatable dishes in the house. After the initial preparations, cooking, laying the table, etc. how much time does it take to eat the food? Hardly any time. In the same manner, sitting on the seat of meditation is like taking food. You just straightaway start. Otherwise, you sit on the dining table and raw rice is kept in front of you. Rather, paddy is kept. You have to pound it, clean it, cook it, add spices etc.. So, meditation is like this. Preparations are extremely important. So, what preparation will we do today? We took up the aspect called self discipline, and how it is necessary to change the old habits of the mind. The old habit of, whatever I want to do, the way I want to do, that alone I will do and that is all. It is not like that. With this understanding, we go to the next step. We have two components in our personality. One is matter. Second is consciousness. When our meditation is basically matter oriented, we will be trying throughout our lives to control and win over matter. So that matter does not change. But, the fact of the matter is that matter does change. Because, wherever there is 'prakruti', 'vikruti' is bound to be. Without 'vikruti', 'prakruti' cannot exist. That is the nature.

Therefore, if we spend our whole life only in controlling matter, we will only end up in more and more frustration because of failure, and in more and more arrogance because of success. When we end up in failure, we get depression, or we become destructive.

When we become successful concerning matter, we become arrogant and we have the audacity to bless or curse somebody!

Therefore, one aspect of our meditation is matter oriented and the second is consciousness oriented. We have to understand that this is the one big difference between the Samkhya Yoga of Kapila Maharshi and Vedanta. In the Samkhya philosophy, consciousness and matter are different from each other, independent of each other.

Let Meditation Happen

But, in the case of Vedanta Shastra, this is not accepted. In Vedanta Shastra it is said that matter, 'prakruti', potentiality or 'maya' is 100% dependant on 'purusha' or consciousness. This potentiality cannot exist independently. Like, my power of speech. My power of speech cannot exist apart from me and independent of me. In the same manner, this power of speech because of which you know me, this is definitely other than me. So, if it is other, does it mean it is independent?

No.

Therefore, when we give importance to potentiality, matter, on one side and the consciousness on the other side, then alone our spiritual progress will go systematically. One person wanted to take part in the Olympics. He asked what the qualifications were. The qualifications were that you should have two legs. He had two legs. But, one had elephantitis and the other had polio. So, if one leg is thick and the other thin, there will be a complete imbalance in his personality. In the same manner, if we practice only matter, matter, matter, Or only yoga, yoga, yoga, then that aspect of our personality will have elephantitis and as a result, knowledge, understanding will be zero. It will have polio and vice versa. If we are only talking Vedanta and never practicing Vedanta, then we only become scholars. We can give lectures, but as far as our own life is concerned, it is totally a flop show.

Therefore, we have to strike a perfect and beautiful balance between knowledge and wisdom on one side and control and discipline on the other. If these two things are perfectly attained, then alone will your meditation be a success. Now, we are introduced to matter early in our childhood.

What is matter?

Matter starts from the world around us. The world around us includes the place that we stay, the things that we use, clothes, books, pencils, gadgets, everything. So, that is known to us. If a student is really walking the spiritual path, he really has to take care of things in a decent and beautiful manner. Living a life of hotch potch is not a spiritual life. We have to be extremely neat and clean. Everything should be properly kept. Our clothes should be nice. Then we start living in awareness. Otherwise, under the disguise of simplicity, we live shabbily. Shabbiness is not the way to adopt. So, whether it is the things that we have, or the things that we put on, they reflect our personality. "How you dress and how you address declares your character", this is a sentence that has had a great impact on my life since childhood.

How we dress is our external personality. How we address is our internal personality. So, unless there is sufficient perfection, outside and inside, we are not working on the spiritual path. Therefore, we have to slowly change our old habits. The worst habit is dependence on others. When we do things ourselves, it is our necessity. That alone will keep us fit in life. There is this lady, Pushpa Amma, who is always tending to the garden. Someone asked me as to why she does so much. I said that she is selfish. 'No, no, how can you call her selfish?' Because, when she does so, she keeps healthy and happy. Otherwise, you sit in your room the whole day, think and be miserable.

When we keep ourselves busy, occupied in the world, it is our need. The world does not need us. If we live life with this understanding, we are walking the spiritual path. The mind is a problem to us whenever we are free. The more free time we have, the more miserable we are. Misery is expressed in two ways. Violent expression called hysteria. Silent expression called depression. Both these conditions are the luxury of filthy rich people. Those who keep busy physically, don't suffer from misery.

Once I was traveling, and all of a sudden my left shoulder just couldn't move. I wondered what happened. Actually, I used to travel a lot and never exercised. So, one day the shoulder just got frozen. I could not move that hand, for almost a year. So, keeping physically busy keeps us healthy. And therefore, the best way for it is to do our work ourselves. Don't depend on anybody for anything.

Then we will remain alert and fresh. We all have three enemies

Let Meditation Happen

within us. One, laziness, lack of interest in life. A spiritual seeker is one who lives his life full of joy. Laziness can be conquered by changing our lifestyle. So, the best time to do meditation is at 6:00 A.M. Someone once asked me, 'Swamiji, isn't 6:00 o'clock too early for meditation?' No. Starting our day at 6:00 o'clock is the first law.

If this is difficult then you are not cut out for spiritual practice. We have to begin our day, early in the morning. The first requirement in life. When you begin early in the morning, the whole world is sleeping, negative thoughts are at the minimum in the world. In that tranquil, universal atmosphere, when you start your spiritual practice, it becomes conducive. Early morning sleep is the best sleep we ever get.

So, when a useless thing like sleep is best early in the morning, how great will meditation be?

It is the right time to do anything.

So, why waste that beautiful time for sleeping?

To remove the enemy number One, laziness, from our system, this early beginning is a must for every seeker. A lazy person cannot achieve anything in life.

One day, I was watching a cycle race. The participants are extremely inspired when they begin. When you begin anything with inspiration, you are bound to enjoy it. But, when you begin with a burdensome attitude, what can the result be?

When laziness is embedded deep within our system, we do everything half-heartedly.

Nobody is compelling you to meditate. You are doing it on your own. I am teaching you the meditation on my own accord. When I have chosen this myself, on what ground can I justify feeling lazy?

We must do whatever we have to do willingly. Willingness in participation is a tremendous force in life.

If we do not have a strong will, we cannot achieve anything in life.

To remove laziness, invocation of a strong will is necessary. The second enemy is 'nidra', sleep. Sleep is of two types. One is the physiologically required sleep.

That is the healthy sleep which is necessary for every living being. The second aspect of sleep is, after sleep is over, we continue to toss and turn in the bed. That is the unhealthy aspect of sleep. That time we are neither sleeping, nor awake. This aspect of sleep needs to be taken care of with awareness. When we live in awareness, we are alert every moment. When we are not alert, we miss even a few seconds of an incident, and then try to join the pieces without the proper links in between. Please remember , we have to catch in one go. Inspired words and moments are never repeated. The moment repeatability comes, it becomes a prepared lecture. On the spiritual path, repetition is a mechanical existence, which is wrong.

We like repetition because we are not alert. We must develop the faculty of remaining alert and vigilant. Third enemy is 'pramad', making the same mistake again and again. Thus, we become experts in doing the wrong things, perfectly well. These three things have to be taken into account as a preparation for meditation. Laziness must disappear. There must be an alertness.

When alertness is absent, many seekers go to sleep while meditating. It is necessary to remain alert and not go to sleep.

Third and most important, we must not repeat the same mistake again and again. The biggest mistake that we keep making, is mistaking ourselves to be the body!

Now, this mistake we have been doing every day, every moment.

So the first goal to be reached is body dis identification. The reason why I am unable to get into yoga, asanas, is this. The moment I start, I realize that I am once again getting body oriented. The goal of our life is to discard body identification. When we remain in awareness, we will not repeat this same mistake. There are two 'sadhanas' to be practiced. 'Bahirang sadhana' and 'Antarang sadhana' 'Bahirang sadhana is how we deal with the outer world.

Our dealing with the outer world should be such that we remain undisturbed, alert, quiet and awake. That is the quality of mind required for arriving at the seat of meditation. This is the external principle of interacting with the world in such a manner that our

Let Meditation Happen

internal peace is not compromised. This is the 'yama' of yoga sutras.

'Antarang sadhana', inner discipline. The three enemies which destroy our inner peace are:
1] Laziness
2] Unhealthy sleep
3] Repeating the same mistake again and again.

In this manner, when we become overall fresh and aware, then meditation is a possibility. Alertness, brightness means reaching closer to the light of consciousness. I was giving a lecture once and the person in charge was recording it. There were too many bright lights and I asked them to reduce the lights. 'No, no Swamiji, we need these lights for recording.' 'I know how to record,' I said, but he did not listen. Not listening is the rule. I said OK as one of us had to listen. Then we did the whole recording. When we saw it later, everything was white. The background was white. My face, beard, clothes, everything was white, as though a ghost was talking.

'Swamiji, how did this happen?'

'This happened because of your wisdom. When I asked you to reduce the lights, you would not listen.' 'But, I thought......' 'Who asked you to think? You were asked to switch off the lights.'

So, when you are closer to the light of consciousness, you remain alert. When you are away from the light of consciousness, you remain dull. We don't know how wrong we are going, most of us are living in sleep.

Someone once asked me, 'Swamiji, what is the reason that mahatmas do not get disturbed when somebody praises them or abuses them?' What is the secret, that they can remain so cool?

I told him, 'Suppose your wife is sleeping, and in her sleep she says, I love you, or I am going to kill you. You are awake and you know that she is merely talking in her sleep. Therefore, you will laugh it off.' In the same manner, wise people know that worldly people are talking in their sleep. So, whether they are praised or condemned, it makes no difference.' The wise man is awakened to reality. We are most of the time, living in waking sleep. We are not aware. Meditation is all time awareness in manifestation. No living life on the ground is taken for granted. Never take a single moment in life for granted. Our life is indisciplined. So we keep shuttling between dullness and awareness. I am supplying you with the food which you need. You don't have to worry about calories, cholesterol, about anything. Just go ahead and eat it. So, these meditations are systematically planned out for your upliftment. Go ahead and give it your best shot. My aim is not to give you only knowledge. Knowledge you already have. What is required is translation of that knowledge in life, to experience the truth. All knowledge must be translated in experience. Every day, every moment is meditation. We live in meditation. This living in meditation, is real meditation. It is not a drill of a military sergeant, 'All together, Meditate!' No.

The expression of the blissful conscious self through us, is meditation. In and through all the expressions of life. Whether we are sitting, talking or we are silent. This poise with which we live, determines to what extent we have reached the deep heights in meditation. More awareness. Less agitation.

How do you know whether you are living in awareness?

The world and matter will not matter much in our life. We have had enough comforts in our life. I don't think any of us was born on the road or lived as a beggar. We all have lived a very comfortable life. Comforts of life we have already enjoyed.

What has it given us?

Have we discovered fulfillment?

If not, why not give ourselves another chance?

Instead of living in comfort, why not live in awareness. Let us give it a chance. We will then see, that living in awareness is more rewarding than living in comfort. Living in awareness leads to freedom. Living in comforts leads to bondage. Living in awareness, dependence is zero. Living in comforts, dependence is 100%. We have to live with this awareness. Do not concentrate anywhere. This is one of the most essential things that we have to get into our system.

Let Meditation Happen

Don't live a life of intense concentration.
Relax and remain aware. Concentration is not on the self.
Concentration is on others. Awareness is on the self.
In awareness, we drop matter.
In concentration we hold onto matter.
Do this experiment right away.
Concentrate on the centre of your chest.
You will see that you are locked up in the body.
Second experiment.
Take the position of space.
Remain as space.
Space is the supporter of everything but is not influenced by anything.

It does not have shape and form, so our shape and form disappear.
When shape and form disappear, concentration is zero.
Living in this awareness, is spiritual life.

If you happen to develop any pressure in any part of the body, then you are going the wrong way. You are concentrating and getting lost in matter.

Be aware of this and drop it immediately.
Breathe deeper slowly. Don't do anything suddenly.
Get into activity slowly and gracefully.

✦ ✦ ✦

MEDITATION 3

Matter and conscious existence, the difference between these two appears to be on account of the expression of manifestation.

When the difference between these two disappears, it is called realization.

When I know an object, that which is known, is inert.

I know this book. But, the book does not know me.

In me, knowledge and existence, both are expressing themselves together.

So, what is my experience, about myself?

That I am.

Conscious existence.

Being is existence. Being aware is consciousness.

So, in us, the experiencer, the consciousness and existence are not separated.

But, in the experience, 'This is a book', I am aware of being. This is also an experience. And 'This is a book', is also an experience.

So, what is the difference between these two experiences?

In the second experience, the book is recognized as mere existence, therefore it is only inert. The touch of consciousness is not seen in the book. So, the book cannot know me. I know the book, this is the first step.

Now, when we become aware of the first phenomena, then we come to the point of, 'Who is practicing meditation?'

The mere matter?

The mere world?

Or the absolute conscious blissful existence?

One is the world.

Second is experiencer of the world.

Third is the absolute conscious blissful existence.

In matter, book, only existence.

Knower that I am, conscious existence.

Let Meditation Happen

The ultimate truth that is, conscious blissful existence.

So, in matter alone, there is no 'samsara', no relativity, because there is no knower, known difference.

In the conscious blissful existence there is no 'samsara' or relativity because it is the absolute.

So, where is the 'samsara'?

The 'samsara', is in the conscious existence, the experiencer of the world, as we are.

Now, what is the instrument by which the experience is experienced?

Is it the eyes that are seeing, or is it the mind behind the eyes that is seeing?

Is it the lips that are talking, or is it the mind behind the lips that is talking?

Now, secondly, is it the inert mind that is seeing or is it the enlivened mind that is seeing, by the light of reflected consciousness?

So, it is not just the mind, but the mind that is reflecting the light of consciousness, that takes the position of the experiencer.

This experiencer is therefore, enlivened mind by the light of reflected consciousness and this enlivened mind has the notion of I versus not I.

This is a book.

But, I am the knower of the book.

The enlivened mind dichotomies, in this manner, into a bifurcation, separation, between the knower, the conscious one and the known, the inert one.

Therefore, all spiritual practice is working on two levels.

1] Working on the mind which is coming in contact with the world.

2] Working on this I notion, who is experiencing the world.

Yoga Shastra talks about working on the mind. The experiencer of the world is taken for granted.

Yoga Shastra talks about controlling our thoughts.

Control of thoughts becomes our primary concern.

Let Meditation Happen

Control of the mind is for one purpose only. To discard body identification.

This is done by wisdom and application of wisdom in one's life.

Wisdom is gained through inquiry and understanding, appreciation and evaluation of our own experiences.

Application is practiced through Yoga, on the seat of meditation.

Having clarity of goal and a road map are very important.

When we have to go to a friends place, we ask for his address. Then we ask him for directions.

We then have to withdraw from the world and concentrate on driving, so that we don't meet with an accident.

Sufficient petrol is needed in the car.

We cannot sleep while driving.

So, too, instructions are needed when we begin meditation.

1) The destination should be clear: body disidentification and inquiry about the soul, the jiva.
2) The roadmap is two ways. Dealing with the world and dealing with ourselves.

We can go away from the world, to protect ourselves from the world.

But, where can we run away from ourselves?

Therefore, the first spiritual practice is, live in the world in such a manner that we do not react to anything and our mind remains equipoised.

So, how must we take care of ourselves?

Do not give yourself any free time.

Keep busy.

Remember the Lord's name.

When this is done in our daily routine, we will be given a visa to enter on the seat of meditation.

So, a few instructions for the seeker.

1] He/she must have a particular time of the day which is fixed for meditation.

The mind has this habit forming tendency. When we practice

Let Meditation Happen

meditation for a few weeks, then when that particular time will come, the mind will be oriented for meditation.
Regularity is the secret of success in life.
Just as we cannot take a bottle of tonic in one go.
We have to take a small dose every day.
In the same manner, we have to practice meditation on a daily basis.
So, which time is the best for meditation?
That time which is ours.
Not the time which is allotted to someone else.
So, what is the right time?
Early in the morning. That time is our own.

2] If it is possible, do not share your asana with anyone.
Keep it as though it is auspicious and sanctified.
No other worldly indulgence or talk should be indulged in, on that asana. Like having a cup of tea, food etc..
That gives away the sanctity associated with meditation.

3] The room or place where we practice meditation should not be cluttered with too many objects. Every object will send its own quota of disturbances.
So, let us not have a tendency to accumulate things.

4] The asana should not be very hard, nor very soft.
It should be sufficiently soft to sit firmly.
If the asana is too soft, we will get sunk in it and our back will not be straight.
Keeping the back straight has the following benefits. We will not feel sleepy.
Understanding will be quick.
We will be able to balance our body for a longer period of time.

5] Your mood is very important. When you sit for meditation, are you dragging yourself?
Your willingness and cheerfulness is crucial to the progress you make in meditation.

6] You could have a picture of the Lord, idol or it could be nothing, a plain wall, in front of you. Many a seeker has a fear when they sit for meditation. Fear is expressed when they start cracking their joints. Whenever you have a fear, you will hold onto something. If there is nothing, you will hold your own hands. If you try to sleep in 'shavasana', legs and hands separated, you will not be able to sleep. You have to hold onto something. Either a pillow, blanket, or yourself. So, to remove this deep set fear, two things are to be remembered.
a] In our heart is seated our beloved Lord. He is protecting us. He is taking care of us. We are not alone.
b] Our Guru or teacher is guiding us from within.

Now there is assurance.

7] Notice that all thoughts begin when you become some body. So when you become a mother, thoughts of children come naturally. Whenever you become somebody, that becoming is the point of origin of all thoughts.

In just being, no thoughts are possible.

The moment we become somebody, a series of thoughts are born.

Thoughts are of three kinds.

A] About memories of the past. Travelling in the memory lane.

B] Solving the non existent problems of the future. What is technically termed as worry.

C] Thoughts of comparison in the present. Labelling, evaluation.

These three kind of thoughts persecute us on the seat of meditation.

What can be done about them?

A very simple technique.

A] Block the past. So, the memory lane is closed. This is done by becoming Mr. Nobody.

Let Meditation Happen

What is the meaning of somebody? Somebody is the sum total of the past.
When we become nobody, no thoughts will trouble us about the past.

B] The future has to be blocked. How? Do not decide what you will do after meditation.
Do not decide for how long you are going to sit for meditation.
Do not plan anything.

C] To stop the comparison process, we have to be fully involved in the meditation. If we do it half heartedly then we will not progress or disappear into it. To eradicate half heartedness, we should think that this moment is the last moment of our life.

Then we will know that the truth is now or never. The truth is not experienced in a future period of time. It is not experienced in the distant land of mountains.

No! It is now and here.

Imagine that there is nothing left to be achieved in the world. Our relationship with the world is over.

Now, let us try it out.

Sit properly.

You are cheerful and happy.

In your heart is your beloved Lord and the Guru.

You are Mr. Nobody.

There are no plans for after meditation.

Now, you are here 100%.

With this simple preparation, watch your body.

The base has become firm.

The body is vertically steady.

The weight of the body has distinctly increased on the base of the spine, at the pin bones.

The body is slowly and steadily being dropped from the mind.

Do not concentrate on any part of the body.

Tension patches will slowly disappear from the various parts of the body.

The breathing is extremely slow and shallow.

Now take the position that the illuminator who is illuminating the body, is other than the body. Therefore, be formless and do not be caged inside the body.

So, there is no part in the body, from top to toe, where there is any internal pressure.

You are not pulling inside yourself.

Remain relaxed.

If you want, relax the body more and more.

Full relaxation of the body is erasing the shape of the body from the mind.

So, the body is dropped and the mind is now free and formless.

When any thought takes you for a ride, and when you recognize that, trace back as to where it began. You will come to know, that at the beginning , there was somebody.

So, being has taken the position of becoming and somebody was present.

Therefore, this has to be ingrained in our understanding.

Without 'somebody', thoughts cannot erupt.

Somebody is born with body identification.

Don't fight with the mind.

Don't get carried away with any thought.

Slowly increase the depth of your breathing.

Move your toes and fingers.

Feel the body.

Offer everything to the Lord.

Do not carry the load of the experience with you.

✦ ✦ ✦

MEDITATION 4

The fundamental goal of our life is, body disidentification without sleeping or death.

What exactly does it mean? Let us see with an example.

When an artist or sculptor is working on a project, he is so lost doing that job, that he is not even aware of his body. He is functioning through the body but he is no more functioning as the body. Therefore, for him, the body will not be an impediment. It will not be an obstacle.

Body dis identification means that body is not the only concern in life.

When we come on the seat of meditation, we prepare external things.

Asana is prepared properly.

Idol is properly kept.

Everything is neat and clean.

We close all the doors and windows and we are in front of our Lord.

After this, we chant some prayer.

When we chant, the Guru or the Lord is the point of focus.

So, by the prayer, we withdraw from the body, to a great extent.

After this, we have to keep the body on the seat, in such a manner, that we no longer have to make any efforts to keep the body on the seat.

Whenever efforts are required, we are not comfortable.

Patanjali Maharshi describes the asana to be 'sthira sukham asanam'.

Effortlessly blissful.

Asanam is not only posture. It is being.

Blissful, flawless, undisturbed being.

We have to get rid of the attention towards the body.

We have to keep the body on the asana and forget about it.

Let Meditation Happen

When we sleep, we keep the body on the bed, cover it properly and then forget about it.

If this step is not taken, our mind will only be running in the gross world.

Therefore, body disidentification means, the gross world and the body are no more troubling us.

Now, as Mr.Nobody, we discard the total gross world along with its problems, achievements, etc..

Everything related to the body is deleted.

This posture that we are sitting in, is a geometrically stable posture.

All three sides are equal like an equilateral triangle or a cone.

The distance between the knees, between the spine end and knees and the neck, all these are approximately equal.

Any structure is stable, if the center of gravity lands exactly in the center.

The center of gravity of our body must land on the two pin bones, which are touching the floor.

The pin bones are medically called, Ischai points.

The pelvic bone is touching the floor at these two points, and the anus opening is in between.

It is this particular point at the base of our body, on these points, that the body weight must land.

You may open up your legs, you may close them, whatever may be required, but see that the weight of the body lands on these two pin bones.

It is extremely necessary.

You have to subjectively do that.

Nobody can help you.

Now, one or two suggestions for that.

We have to get rid of the attention towards the body.

We have to keep the body on the asana and forget about it.

When we sleep, we keep the body on the bed, cover it properly and then forget about it.

If this step is not taken, our mind will only be running in the

Let Meditation Happen

gross world.

Therefore, body disidentification means, the gross world and the body are no more troubling us.

Now, as Mr.Nobody, we discard the total gross world along with its problems, achievements, etc..

Everything related to the body is deleted.

This posture that we are sitting in, is a geometrically stable posture.

All three sides are equal like an equilateral triangle or a cone.

The distance between the knees, between the spine end and knees and the neck, all these are approximately equal.

Any structure is stable, if the center of gravity lands exactly in the center.

The center of gravity of our body must land on the two pin bones, which are touching the floor.

The pin bones are medically called, Ischai points.

The pelvic bone is touching the floor at these two points, and the anus opening is in between.

It is this particular point at the base of our body, on these points, that the body weight must land.

You may open up your legs, you may close them, whatever may be required, but see that the weight of the body lands on these two pin bones.

It is extremely necessary.

You have to subjectively do that.

Nobody can help you.

Now, one or two suggestions for that.

1] You could open up the legs a little so that weight doesn't land on the calf muscles or any other part of the leg.

2] Don't sit at exactly a 90 degree angle. If you sit at 90 degree angle, you will have the fear of falling back. So, reduce the angle by maybe one quarter, so that the weight of the body lands exactly on the two pin bones. If this aspect is not properly taken care of, then your legs may go to sleep. Blood circulation gets hampered when there is excessive weight on

Let Meditation Happen

the legs.

3] Next come the hands. If you keep your hands on the knees, like many people do, or maybe you have seen in a picture. It is good for taking a picture but it is not advised in practical. When you sit like this, after some time, the hands pull the body forward and the center of gravity gets displaced. Then, one may feel sleepy or get tired.

Therefore, keep your hands like this. Either the lower three fingers are interlocked, index finger to index finger and thumb to thumb and put them in your lap.

This is one way.

Second way is, put your left palm below and right palm above. Touch the thumbs together and keep your hands on your lap. When the hands are on your lap, the center of gravity does not get disturbed.

There is no tension on the shoulders.

Now, this has become a perfect structure, where no pull or push is felt. So, the ideal posture has three aspects.

A] Base is firm.

B] Vertically the body is steady.

C] Body is fully relaxed.

Now the first two things have happened.

The third thing is relaxing the body fully.

This we have to start from the top and go till the toe, part by part.

Now, you are seated properly.

Remind yourself of the psychological adjustments every time.

You are cheerful and happy.

You are doing this willingly. There is no compulsion.

You are not obliging the teacher or the world.

You are nobody.

You have no plans for after meditation.

The Lord is in your heart.

Your teacher protects and guides you from within.

Let Meditation Happen

With these adjustments, we are in the present.
Now get fully involved without any seriousness.
So, we will start giving instructions to the body.
We will relax.
You don't worry about how it will happen.
Don't come between my instructions and the body.
You get out.
Relax the head muscles.
Relax the forehead.
Relax the eyebrows.
Relax the eyeballs.
Relax the eyelids. Don't have them half open, half closed.
Relax the nose.
Relax the lips.
Relax the chin.
Relax the face muscles.
Relax the ears.
Relax relax-relax.
Relax the neck from the front, sides and the back.
Hang down the shoulders, they are unnecessarily lifted up.
Relax the shoulder joints.
Relax the upper arms.
Relax the elbows.
Relax the lower arms.
Relax the wrist.
Relax the palms.
Relax the fingers.
Relax relax-relax.
Now take a small break. Observe that the body is now divided in two parts.
Relaxed and not yet relaxed.
The relaxed portion has minimum muscle tone.
No tension.
The hands are heavily felt on the lap.

Let Meditation Happen

The index finger and thumb are as if, hard against each other.
The weight of this portion is felt on the lap.
The remaining body still has the muscle tone.
Now, come to the shoulders again.
Now we will relax the main trunk and the lower limbs.
From the throat right up to the base.
From the shoulder joint right up to the hip joint.
From the neck right up to the pin bones.
Relax the chest muscles.
The sides, upper back.
Relax relax-relax.
Relax the abdomen, stomach, and below up to the floor.
Relax from the rib cage up to the hip joints.
Relax from the upper back downwards. Go along the spine.
Go downwards. Relax up to the pin bones.
You may experience pulsation on these pin bones.
The weight of the body has increased now, on these two points.
Relax the hips.
Relax the thighs.
Relax the knees.
Relax the calf muscles.
Relax the ankles.
Relax the heels up to the toes.
Now, the body is fully relaxed.
Now, you, as if, walk out of the body.
  Like there may be many bodies around you, so, this is one body which we call I or ours.
  But, in fact, there is no difference. Whether we see other bodies or our own body.
  Now, remaining outside the body, take the front view of the body.
The top, forehead, eyebrows.
Go downwards slowly slowly. Part by part.
If you come across any patch of tension, Relax.
Now, go to the right side of the body.

Let Meditation Happen

Don't forget that you are outside the body.
Now, take the right view of the body.
The right side of the head.
The right ear.
The right side of the neck.
The right shoulder.
Thus, go part by part.
Up to the hip joints.
Relax relax relax
Now, go to the back side of the body.
See the top, backside of head, neck, shoulder blades.
Go downwards upto the waist.
Relax if you come across any patch of tension.
Go to the left side.
You will observe a little more tension on the left side, as the other three sides are now fully relaxed.
So, repeat the process.
See the left side of the head.
The left ear.
Go downwards slowly.
See the left arm.
The left elbow.
Left hip joint.
Left knee.
Etc..
Relax relax relax.
Now come to the front again.
Now the body is firm at the base.
Vertically steady.
Relaxed totally.
Actually, it is not the body that is relaxed.
It is the mind that has given up the shape of the body.
Hence, the mind is no more carrying the weight of the body.
The shape and form of the body, is slowly becoming hazy and

Let Meditation Happen

non distinct.

The contour line of the body is almost vanished.

The concept of inside or outside the body, is now meaningless.

When the concept of inside or outside is gone, there cannot be any concentration anywhere.

Space is not concentrated anywhere.

In the same manner, the awareness that we are, is without any concentration.

Be extremely vigilant so that you do not create any tension or pressure in the head.

You are not in the body.

The body is in you.

Not only one body.

All the bodies.

All the names and forms.

The breathing is extremely slow.

The nasal metabolic rate has fallen.

Minimum oxygen requirement.

Slow and shallow breathing.

If the breathing starts becoming deep, then you are marching towards sleep.

If the breathing becomes fast, you are marching towards body identification.

Thus, slow and shallow breathing is last but one step and the ultimate will be 'kevala kumbhaka', when breathing is suspended.

Just remain aware of this bodyless experience.

Start breathing deeper, slowly.

Move your toes and fingers. Offer everything to the Lord.

✦✦✦

MEDITATION 5

Sound has its effect on our mind in two ways.

In exciting the mind as well as in quietening the mind.

When the theme entertained by sound, is the world, then the mind gets excited, disturbed, by sounds.

If the theme entertained by the mind is divinity, the absolute, the real, then the mind gets quietened.

When you listen to various compositions in Sanskrit language, by great masters, you become calm.

So make it a point to chant a stotra everyday, when you sit for meditation. Don't chant the same mantra or stotra everyday. If you do that, it will become mechanical.

One day you could chant the guru stotra, sadhana panchakam etc..

In this manner, we remain alert and fully involved.

Otherwise laziness sets in.

When we sit for meditation, the goal is the first thing that should come to our mind.

Why are we sitting?

Do we want to become an expert in meditation, so that we can teach others?

Start a meditation studio?

Or is it so that we may have one more discussion topic to talk about?

Like in many big houses, they have discussion topics.

They have nothing to talk about.

So, people have discussion topics, when they have nothing to talk about.

Therefore, the goal has to be clear.

We have to get rid of body identification.

Like our shoes, vehicles, help us to reach a destination, they are not the goal.

Like a language. The language is only a means. It doesn't matter

Let Meditation Happen

in which language you talk. What matters is what you say.

Are you able to communicate or do you confuse people, under the disguise of communication?

Therefore, meditation is only a means.

The goal is body disidentification.

Unless we have the goal firmly, clearly and deeply rooted in our mind, we will not be able to practice meditation with clarity.

Or else, we will keep on sitting everyday, and after five-ten years, we will complain that nothing has happened.

I have come across many people who face this problem.

Some people go to Vipassana meditation.

I am not against any particular practice.

Do whatever you like.

We are here to understand.

So, after going there for years together, they say, 'Swamiji, we have been doing this for so many years, but actually, nothing has happened. On the contrary, more funny behaviour has started. Anger and all that has started.'.

Now this happens when we overdo things.

Meditation is not a forced discipline on the mind but it is a wise approach to life.

The 'kumbhaka' is another practice that we force on ourselves.

Normally, we do not hold our breath.

Breathing is a continuous process.

When we take air inside and hold it for a particular time, breathe out and again hold, this creates confusion in the mind.

Our goal is to get rid of the body from the mind.

But, when we practice this breathing and holding of the breath, it becomes only an exertion.

Why do we practice pranayama?

Because we feel fresh?

Feeling fresh is not the purpose of meditation.

Therefore, let us be clear in our understanding.

Or else, we take air inside, bombard the 'kumbhaka' on the

Let Meditation Happen

'mooladhara chakra', so that it opens.

Then you start chanting 'Om'. And let the sound waves be directed towards the 'mooladhara'. Then it will open.

So, we get more and more body oriented.

Instead of getting out of the body.

We get buried in it.

Keeping body identification intact, and imagining that the mind will be free from body oriented thoughts, is absolutely impossible.

Imagine that you are carrying a bag with a fish in it.

If you think that it will not smell, it is not possible.

In the same manner, as long as we are identified with the body, the smell of the body will be reflected in the thoughts, in the mind.

If the body has pain somewhere, our meditation will be painful.

If you have a toothache and you sit for meditation, all the attention will be on the toothache.

We have learnt the body relaxation technique.

What exactly happens when we relax?

Understanding this relaxation is very important, or else, we will only be imagining that we are doing meditation.

Say I have a bag.

In the bag, there is a paper weight.

I lift the bag along with the paper weight.

Now, who has the tension?

Does the paper weight have the tension, or is it the walls of the bag that have tension?

When we are told, to relax the body, it means that we relax the paper weight.

But, the paper weight was not tense anyway.

So, how can we relax it?

Body never has tension.

It is the mind which has the tension, because in the bag of the mind, is the pumpkin of the body.

This is how it is.

So, when we keep the bag along with the content on the floor, who is relaxed?

It is the bag and not the content.

Because the content was not tense in the first place.

So, when we relax the body, part by part, what we do is, slowly and steadily, we bring the bag closer to the floor.

When we begin from the top, we start bringing the bag, closer to the floor, and slowly start leaving it.

Slowly steadily.

And when the last bit of relaxation is complete, it means that the mind has fully dropped the body.

Relaxation is always of the mind and never of the body.

We have to say, 'relax the body', as we are not yet clear about where the tension is.

Our attention is all the time, only on the body.

We have to be told, 'relax your body'.

In fact, it is the mind that relaxes.

So, when the body is relaxed, that is, the mind is relaxed, then what happens?

Once again take the example of the bag.

If you see the base of the bag, it has taken the shape of the paper weight.

Now, if we replace the paper weight with a mobile phone, the bag will take the shape of the phone.

In the same manner, the total mind, when it gets identified with a particular body,

that particular shape of the body, is taken by the mind.

The individuality remains as long as the shape of the body in the mind is valid.

After the mind drops body identification, as in the case of deep sleep, the mind again reverts back to the formless, infinite status.

Therefore, the mind is not carrying the load of the shape of the particular body.

Weight is not always in terms of gravitational force. Weight is also in terms of shape.

Let Meditation Happen

If you take a piece of cloth which is very light.

If you hold it in your hand, for 4-5 hours, the hand will start paining, after some time.

Because the hand has taken the particular shape for a long period of time.

So, unless the mind is freed from the shape of the body, the mind cannot think of something higher than the body.

We will constantly be shunting through body related activities. Waking, dream, deep sleep or Samadhi.

One day, a doctor, very well educated, he was after me to make him experience 'Nirvikalpa Samadhi.'

I asked him, 'Suppose I make you experience that. What next? Are you going to remain in that state, eternally?'

'No, but I want to experience it.'

I told him that just as waking comes and goes, dream comes and goes, sleep comes and goes, so also Samadhi comes and goes.

According to our scriptures, every one of us, goes through 'Nirvikalpa Samadhi', hundred times a day.

Everyone.

But we are not aware of it.

We recognize the waking experience.

We recognize the dream experience.

We recognize the sleep experience.

But, we do not recognize Samadhi.

Although we go through the experience, we do not know it.

Once I went to England.

One man was to come to receive me, whom I had never seen before.

He was informed that he would recognize me as I have a different dress, beard etc..

My luggage came late and another Swami went out before me.

You know, there are many Swamis these days.

So, the man gave him the flowers and garland etc..

The swami asked him about who had sent him and they realized that he was not the right Swami.

So, when I went out, he apologized profusely and regretted that he had no garland for me!

Although there is a person, but if we do not know, we miss him.

In the same manner, although we go through 'Nirvikalpa samadhi', we miss it.

Another important fact, is that every gain is through knowledge.

Suppose we purchase a lottery ticket.

We have won the lottery but if we do not know it, that is we do not check it, then the gain is not ours.

Gain is always through knowledge.

Never through action.

In the same manner, the body is ours only if it is included in the mind.

If it is dropped from the mind, it is not ours.

We can start our journey from where we are.

We are in the body,

so, we must start from the body.

We keep the body in such a manner, that it is 'sthira sukham asanam'.

The experience of 'sukham'.

The experience of happiness.

The experience of bliss.

Is undisturbed.

A particular posture is not necessarily the asanam.

It is not 'sthira asanam sukham'.

No. It is 'sthira sukham asanam'.

If we have any painful experience, we will be constantly disturbed.

Our attention should be on this blissful disposition.

Without much effort, the body is now still.

Patanjali Maharshi gives us two practices by which flawless bliss can be attained effortlessly.

1] Prayatna shaithilya.

2] Ananta samapatti.

Let Meditation Happen

We are blissful when we do not struggle.

Whenever there is effort, struggle, we are not normal.

If we have to put in a lot of efforts to hear, because of impaired hearing, then we get tired very quickly.

We become irritable.

Efforts put in for listening, tire us.

In the same manner, when we sit for meditation, with a lot of effort, after few minutes, the fidgeting starts.

So, a method of effortlessness has to be adopted.

When the center of gravity remains in the center, the body does not get displaced, and will remain in the same posture without any effort.

That is 'prayatna shaithilya'.

Otherwise all our energy will dissipate only in maintaining the posture.

'Oh, but they say, that this disease will be cured by this posture'.

'Yes, what they say is right. But, once again, what is the goal of our meditation?'

As a disease curative method or for God realization?

If the goal is clear, there won't be any ambiguity or arguments in thinking.

If our goal is practicing yoga for health purposes, then the very start is different.

Suppose we are cooking food.

Are we cooking it for a beggar?

Or are we cooking it as 'naivedyam' for the Lord?

So, the purpose makes the difference.

If we are satisfied, that after doing pranayama, our lungs are clear and we feel fresh, healthy and energetic, or after doing this asana, my back pain is gone, then it is fine.

But, do we make a profession out of it?

If I have a headache and I take an aspirin.

The headache goes away.

So, should I say that everybody should take aspirin?

No. the purpose is not the advertisement of aspirin.
Our purpose is, take it and be busy with your job.
In the same manner, all yogic practices are meant for freedom from body identification.
When we sit in the posture as described by me earlier, one problem still remains.
Because of the mind in the shape of the body, there is a tone in the muscles of the body.
That muscle tone, is nothing but the mind in a particular shape.
When we relax the body, the muscle tone goes away.
In other words, the mind has discarded the shape of the body.
There are two pots.
One in the shape of a conical flask and another in the shape of a test tube.
In these two pots, space will have two different shapes.
When the pots break, what will happen to the two shapes?
They will merge in the total space.
Total space is shapeless, although supporting all shapes.
In the same manner, the mind is also an element.
Mind is the sixth sense organ.
External objects- sound, form, touch, taste and smell.
They are comprehended by the five sense organs respectively.
The ear, eyes, skin, tongue and nose.
Then the inner experiences are supported by the inner instrument.
If the inner instrument is conditioned by the body,
it will always have the biasness and influence of the body form.
But, when the mind drops the body shape, merges with the total mind,
then there is no concept of inside and outside.
When this concept of inside and outside is over,
the illusion of knower, known,
experiencer, experienced,
this duality disappears.
Now, there is only knowledge.

Without the division of knower and known.
Knowledge with division of knower known is mind.
Knowledge without the dichotomy of knower known is consciousness.

There is nothing to discuss or understand. Just be alert lest we go to sleep.

Be vigilant that there is no pressure inside the body, particularly the head.

You are not inside the head.

When thoughts appear, we see that they begin with somebody.

Immediately drop that identity.

That somebody.

We are like space.

All bodies are in the space.

Space is not in the body.

Pot space appears to be inside the pot.

Actually it is not because the pot space is created by the walls of the pot.

These walls are in the total space, so the pot space is inside the pot.

The separateness from the total space is only on account of excessive pre-occupation with the pot walls.

When the body is fully dropped from the mind,
there is neither sleep nor death,
What remains is pure consciousness.

Whatever we have given importance to, positive or negative,
that becomes the source of disturbance in the mind.

We have to come out of likes and dislikes, consciously.

When there is body disidentification, no sleep.

Breathing remains slow and shallow.

With long practice this breathing comes to a complete halt without death.

This is called 'kevala kumbhaka'.

This 'kevala kumbhaka' helps us merge in 'kaivalya'.

Let Meditation Happen

Now start breathing deeper.
Move your toes and fingers. The body identification begins.
'Abhivyakti' has become a 'vyakti'.
Principal has become a reality.

✦ ✦ ✦

MEDITATION 6

We have five components in our personality.

We have to have a clear picture about each component.

After having known them clearly, their role, what each component contributes to life and to what extent that component should be allowed to be dominant in our daily lives.

When this knowledge will be clear, we will be able to use them, but not get overpowered by them.

When we get overpowered by them, we become their slaves.

Then tragedy is the only end.

Therefore, let us understand these five components.

The one which is known to everyone and the one we consider to be ourselves, is our gross body or 'annamaya kosha'.

It is made up of 'anna' or food.

The mother eats food and the seed is formed.

The father eats food and the seed is formed.

These two seeds, made out of food, unite together and the result is the baby in the womb of the mother, the foetus.

During the period of growth in the womb, the baby keeps on feeding on the blood of the mother.

After it comes out, it starts feeding on food.

And when this body dies, it becomes food for others.

In this manner, the gross body is made up of food, sustained in food and ultimately becomes food for others.

Therefore the gross body is called 'annamaya kosha'.

Maya means modification. So, food modified is the gross body.

Like wheat modified into a cake is called chappati.

Food modified into a shape is called gross body.

So, this 'annamaya kosha' is our house.

Like when a person goes to a new place, the first thing that he searches for, is a place to stay.

So, we keep searching for a house to stay in.

Let Meditation Happen

In the same manner, we are residing in the body.
So, our body is our house.
We are the residents living in the residence of the body.
This body, like any house, undergoes a lot of changes and modifications through time.
We have to maintain it properly.
We have to clean it.
We have to white wash it.
Keep it functional.
If there are cracks somewhere, they have to be repaired.
In the same manner, we have to keep our body healthy.
The purpose of keeping it neat and clean, is that we are living in it.
I once went somewhere and my host had a huge mansion.
The bedrooms were like huge halls.
I had one –two people with me.
The arrangement for their stay was made in a hotel.
The reason, 'There is no place in the house'.
The whole town could have stayed in that mansion and yet, they did not want those two people to stay there.
This is how we treat our body.
Only for myself.
Not to be shared.
We don't want to serve others.
We only want to use it.
The body has to be used, for ourselves and for serving the world.
These are the two aspects.
If we do not use our body to serve others, we will become the slave of the body.
The body will overpower us.
Now, this body is constantly subject to change.
It is constantly growing older and older with every passing day.
So, our lifestyle has to be such, that we live in this body, keep it functional, in good condition.

Use the body for living and serve the world through the body.
We are in this house, for a short period of time.
We are ever ready to leave the body.
When we deal with the 'annamaya kosha', in this manner,
there will be lesser and lesser problems of the world.
We are residents of the body.
The body is subject to change and modification.
The body is meant for serving others.
A servant has to be a healthy one.
An unhealthy person cannot be a servant.
Suppose I am travelling somewhere with a servant.
I ask him to lift my bag.
'No, Swamiji, I have a backache. I cannot lift heavy things. So can you lift my bag, too?'
That kind of person cannot be a servant.
A servant has to be healthy.
We treat our body with this attitude, because the body is a useful instrument.
We keep it healthy.
Treat it with love.
But, it has to be shared.
By serving the world.
Then alone, we will not be attached to the body.
Now, with this foundation of understanding, we go one step further.
This understanding has to be experienced.
If it is not experienced, it is only intellectual gymnastics.
That is not the purpose of our study or spiritual practice.
This must become our experience.
We work this out on the seat of meditation.
Like we work the whole day.
In the evening we work out our expenses, income, balance etc..
So, when we come on the seat of meditation,
it is something like writing a balance sheet of our daily experiences.

Let Meditation Happen

When we do that, are we convinced that in the days activities, we had become someone other than the body?

Then, our meditation is no longer restricted only on the seat of meditation.

But, it is now practiced throughout the day and night.

This is extremely necessary.

Meditation is aimed at disowning the body and discovering ourselves to be the embodied.

This is the goal.

To achieve this, we have to convert this knowledge into conviction.

All of us live our convictions.

Today, we are fully convinced that we are the body.

Nobody says I am the body but all of us live only as the body.

So, today, as much as we are convinced that we are the body,

our interaction with the world, our contemplation on the position of the body,

should be such, that slowly, with the passage of time,

we are now fully convinced that our identity is someone other than the body.

There are two ways to do this.

1] Analyze every experience.
2] Evaluate this experience on the seat of meditation under created conditions.

The observation will be,

That which is seen is other than the seer.

That which is known, is other than the knower.

The knower is a conscious being.

The known is inert.

We know our body, so we are someone other than the body.

The knower is conscious. So, we are consciousness.

Known is inert. Body is inert.

The known goes on changing, knower remains the same.

The body has been constantly changing from day one, till today.

But, the consciousness has no experience of having undergone

Let Meditation Happen

any change.
    It is the same.
    Observe your body now. It is still.
    Firm at the base.
    Vertically steady.
    Now, there is a clear experience that consciousness is other than the body.
    To further this experience into the absolute, if there are any patches of tension anywhere, relax them.
    Now the shape and form of the body will slowly start disappearing from the knowledge.
    As we start disowning the body,
    erasing it from our mind,
    the breathing in and out becomes extremely slow and shallow.
    As the body disappears, the concept of in and out is no more valid.
    There is no pressure anywhere inside the body, head etc..
    This experience can be viewed in two ways.
    When the body is disowned and disappears from the mind,
    the experience can be said to be of void or nothingness.
    If this is the approach, we are still buried in 'prakruti' or matter.
    If we view this experience as the absence of the gross world, gross body has no influence on our presence.
    This presence which supports both the presence of body identification, gross world as well as their absence.
    Like the rope supports the illusion of snake as well as the absence.
    This eternal presence is the reality.
    Old habits will produce thoughts.
    Don't fight with the thoughts.
    Be indifferent.
    Recognize the presence and absence of body has no impact on our being.
    So is the case with presence or absence of thoughts.
    This eternal presence.

Let Meditation Happen

Slowly take deeper breaths.
Move your toes and fingers.
Offer everything to the lord.
Don't create a concept about this experience.

✦✦✦

MEDITATION 7

The mind has to be oriented for meditation.
The mind is usually oriented for different things, different places.
When we say our mind is not under our control,
what we mean is,
our mind is running from one place to another place,
one time to another time,
one thing to another thing.
This has to be corrected.
Therefore we are told to fix a time for meditation.
So, when we fix a particular time, at least once a day,
the mind becomes oriented for that time.

If it is a regular practice at the same time and same place, it becomes easier for us to take off.

Otherwise, our mind is running in various directions.

Hence, the importance of discipline in reference to a particular time and place.

When we chant a stotra or mantra,
in that invocation, the higher search for something beyond the world is suggested to the mind.

Therefore, through meditation we are not interested in getting anything shorter of reality.

That is the reason, we chant some stotra.

Now, with this preparation,
we collect ourselves as though we were scattered in various places, times, things.

Now, on the seat of meditation, we have to remind ourselves that the goal is freedom from body identification.

The world comes into existence only when we are identified with the body.

With identification, come relational problems.

The basic cause of the mind thinking in relation to the body,

is because, the mind is identified with the body.
Like, when we are identified with our own child.
Our mind will think in terms of the child.
The basic cause is, identification with the mind.
So, for strengthening this knowledge, that body identification is the basic cause of this samsara, we practice meditation.
Two things have to be clear.
1] How do we attain body disidentification?
2] If we have attained it, what will the experience be like?
Because we have not lived consciously as someone functioning through the body,
rather throughout life we have lived as the body.
These two things have to be worked out on the seat of meditation.
Now, we have seen something with reference to the asana.
After this, now asana is with reference to the gross body.
The five components of our personality are
Annamaya kosha
Pranamaya kosha
Manomaya kosha
Vijnayanmaya kosha
Anandamaya kosha
So, we have looked into the annamaya kosha.
When we live in this world, let us not be more and more body oriented.
Let us aim for something higher.
If we remain body oriented, then we live only for the sake of the body.
No. The body is an instrument.
It is to be kept in a perfect and healthy condition.
So that we can use it.
It is not only for the sake of health, but for a higher purpose.
Now, what are the things to be done, with reference to the body.
1] We have to have a perfect control over our diet.
Are we dying because of eating or are we dieting?

Let Meditation Happen

If we eat too much, our system will be spoilt.
If we don't eat at all, that is also wrong.
We have to eat a calculated amount of food three times a day.
It should not be too much or too little.
If our stomach is perfectly OK, most of the organs of the body are OK.
It is just the question of making it a habit.
I had gone to New Zealand and was staying at someone's place for the first time, for two days.
There was a lady who was very fat and she wanted to reduce.
I told her to check with a doctor. Maybe she had thyroid.
She said that her thyroid was fine. But, she did not know the reason why she was not able to reduce her weight.
I asked her to control her intake of food.
So, how do you do that?
Simply by taking a small plate, when you eat.
Don't take a 'parat'[a very big plate].
If you take a huge plate, even if you put a lot, it looks like a little.
Take a small plate, be it breakfast, lunch or dinner.
Make it a rule, not to go for a second helping.
So, by taking these small precautions, we will get controlled automatically.
Initially, it will be difficult.
'Oh, how can I eat only so much?'
Maximum what will happen? You will die?
All problems will be over!
But, remember this, nobody dies out of eating less in this world.
This is the wrong picture that is portrayed,
that people die because of hunger.
No.
People die because of overeating.
Not because of hunger.
In this manner, we consciously take care of the body.
Then on the seat of meditation, we can keep it without getting

tired.
Without getting bulky.
Without getting exhausted.
Now, the second thing.
After we have thus kept the body on the seat,
we will take up the second layer of our personality called as 'pranamaya kosha'.

'Pranamaya kosha' or in simple words, breathing, has got two aspects.

1] To keep the mind and the body together.
Prana is something like glue between the postage stamp
and envelope.
When the glue is there, the envelope and stamp can stay together.
If there is a stamp without the glue, will you keep it?
It will be like keeping one paper on another paper.
It will not stick.
So, for sticking we require glue.
In the same manner, the mind and body remain together,
as long as breathing is going on.
It is very very essential.

2] Supply of required oxygen for the metabolism of the body.
Because we are consuming energy constantly.
This energy is in the form of the food that we eat,
and also in the form of the oxygen that is taken from the
air. So, now we have two diets.
One is the gross diet for the gross body.
For the maintenance of the tissues etc..
Second, the functional energy required for the metabolism,
as well as for the sustenance of life in the body.
This is achieved through the pranamaya kosha.
Controlling this pranamaya kosha is also important.
Like controlling the body.

Let Meditation Happen

With reference to size, activity, involvement etc..
So, we have to control the pranamaya kosha, the breathing.
What do we achieve through pranayama?

1] Whatever food we eat, some part of it is digested and assimilated, the remaining part is thrown out of the body, as it is a toxic waste for the body. It may not be toxic for something else, but for the body in which that garbage is produced, it is toxic waste.

Now, this wastage from the metabolism of the food that is eaten, there are three types of waste.

A] Gross waste
B] Liquid waste
C] Gaseous waste

The gross waste is thrown out of the body as faeces.
The liquid waste is thrown out through urination.
Gaseous waste is thrown out of the system through breathing.
However, as regular and concerned as we are regarding going to the toilet for urination, we are not so with reference to breathing.
As a result, all the gaseous toxins keep on accumulating, in our system.
Where does it go?
Like you know, for the faeces, the storage is the large intestine.
For urine, it is the urinary bladder.
In the same manner, the gaseous toxins go and find place, in between the joints of two bones.
Because, there is place there.
All these toxins keep on accumulating there, and they being toxic, they keep acting on the heads of the bones, the cartilages, the synovial fluid, in the joints.
As time passes, the bones start becoming dry, form gangarines, become rough, synovial fluid dries up.

Let Meditation Happen

As a result, our joint problems begin.
Now, if you break your joint, you will hear a sound.
What is the sound?
The sound is the gas which is accumulated there.
When you break it, the gas is released.
Therefore, we feel relieved whenever we break our joints.
The gas present, makes it tense.
One purpose of pranayama is to clean the body of these gaseous toxins.
Going to the toilet and urinating are routine parts of our daily life.
It is necessary.
Nobody has to be told about it.
In the same manner, pranayama, two times a day, for five minutes each, is helpful in removing all the toxins from the body, on a regular basis.
Morning with an empty stomach.
Evening with an empty stomach.

2] The second advantage of pranayama, is 'nadi shodhanam'.
Cleansing of the body is very important.
We have to clean our body from inside.
Through 'nadi shodhanam'.
Through pranayama.
These breathing sequences are inversely proportionate, to the longevity of life, in a particular body.
If our breathing is very fast, then life is short.
If you see the cats, rats and dogs, they breathe very fast.
Therefore, their life is not very long.
The tortoise breathes once in four minutes. How comfortable.
Therefore, it lives even for 800-900 years in the same body.
So the frequency of breathing has a direct impact on our longevity.
When we breathe fast, body identification is intense.

Therefore, for body dis identification, what will be required?
Very slow breathing.
Then deep breathing.
And shallow breathing.
When we are in deep sleep, breathing is also deep.
When the breathing is very deep, mind gets absorbed in 'prakruti'.
The mind enters a state of complete inertia.
Therefore, when we are sitting for pranayama, we have to be extremely alert and vigilant, About the quality of our breathing.
Are we breathing very fast?
Are we breathing very deep?
Both will not go together.
Either we will be breathing fast, the body identification will take place.
Or we will be breathing deep, then we are going towards sleep.
Therefore, the quality of breathing is of utmost importance.
If you observe, while on the seat of meditation, we breathe 15 times in a minute.
These are the physiological norms of a healthy person.
Through pranayama we have to reduce this as much as possible.
The pranayama which is commonly practiced, in that, we reduce the breathing by holding the breath. That is artificially induced reduction in frequency of breathing.
This may have a good effect but I am teaching you only what I have practiced myself.
It has helped me tremendously.
If something else helps you, you do that.
Now, pranayama is just one very small aspect of meditation.
Like, when we eat, we take a little bit of chutney or pickle.
We don't take large quantities of it.

Once a foreigner saw 'achar' for the first time. He asked me what it was, so I told him, 'This is very tasty and it is my favorite dish'.
I took one small piece and he took a lot.
He then suffered afterwards!
In the same manner, pranayama is a small part of our total meditation.
It is not something that we do all the time.
So, by pranayama we will reduce the frequency of breathing per minute, and increase the depth of breathing while doing pranayma.
These will be the two parameters on which we will be working.

3] Pranayama is a passive process.
When a child is born and if it doesn't cry, they turn the child upside down and splash ice cold water on its back side.
That creates a shiver.
Some kind of sudden thud to the consciousness, by the change in the temperature.
Because of that, there is an initiation of a throb, or 'spanda' in the consciousness.
These are very important observations for the seeker.
The throb of the consciousness, takes place on the sternum, where the diaphragm is attached to the sternum.
The abdomen and chest are separated by a wall called the diaphragm.
The diaphragm is convex from the lung side and concave from the stomach side.
It is a dome shape.
This diaphragm is attached on the rim, along the rib cage of the thorax, at the center it is pulled at it, and is attached to the sternum.
It is where all the ribs surrender in the center of the chest.
It is at this junction that the throb of consciousness, gets initiated.

Let Meditation Happen

When it is initiated, the convex portion of the diaphragm, on the lungs side, becomes flat, because of the throb.

When it becomes flat, there is a vacuum created in the thorax or in the chest.

Because of the vacuum, air gets sucked in.

Therefore, breathing is a passive process.

It is not active.

The thud of consciousness is withdrawn because it is a pulsation.

Expansion, contraction.

So the movement of consciousness, becomes contracted immediately.

When the diaphragm comes to its normal position, it presses on the lungs.

This is how we breathe out.

This is how the breathing process goes on in our system.

Therefore, the breathing and the throb of life or consciousness, are directly related.

When breathing stops, consciousness is not throbbing.

So, when consciousness is not throbbing, it is called death.

Consciousness is there.

But, the throb of consciousness is gone.

When we understand breathing, and our breathing is controlled, that means that we are directly working on the throb of consciousness.

Now we have all the data about pranayama.

Now, I will summarise in a few sentences.

1] The first purpose of pranayama is inner cleansing. Nadi shodhanam.
2] Helping separate the mind from the body. It is because of the prana alone that mind and body are together.

When we practice anything without knowledge, it becomes mechanical.

We do not become engineers.

Let Meditation Happen

A mechanic is able to do a job, better than an engineer, but he continues to be a mechanic throughout life.

In the same manner, if we mechanically go on doing pranayama, without understanding,

it will only remain a mechanical process and we cannot grow mechanically, in life.

Wisdom is not a mechanical by product.

It is an experience gained through enquiry and understanding.

Now, how do we practice it?

First, breathe out. In breathing out we do not do 'bhastrika'.

We breathe out slowly and deeply. Using both nostrils.

Squeeze the stomach muscles, inside upwards.

When we do that, pressure comes on the lungs.

Then, as if we are squeezing out the lungs.

All the air is thrown out.

Second step. We breathe in with both nostrils,

Keeping in view the speed and area where we breathe in.

First of all we will be breathing in the lower lobe of the lungs, which we call stomach.

We will be breathing in the stomach.

When the stomach bulges, it means that it is filled completely with air.

Then we fill the chest with air. The upper lobe of the lungs.

Up to the throat.

So, the complete air tissue, lungs, alveoli, and up to the beginning of windpipe, everything is filled with air.

Very often, many pockets remain, where air has never reached.

Those places remain unutilized.

So, more air means more oxygen.

More oxygen, more exchange of toxins and oxygen replacement.

So this is how it is done.

Then we breathe out.

In breathing out, first we breathe out from the chest.

Let the stomach remain filled.

Let Meditation Happen

Let the chest collapse.
Then consciously we squeeze the stomach, inside upwards.
As much as we can.
This will squeeze out the air fully from our lungs.
The frequency of breathing will slowly and steadily reduce per minute.
This may not happen the first time.
It will happen through practice.
Sometimes it will be that you want to breathe out but the stomach is bulging.
Practice practice practice.
One thing we have to consciously remind ourselves about, is not to hold the breath.
Neither inside nor outside. No holding of the breath.
We are not artificially introducing the 'kumbhaka'.
We are not forcing the bud to open up into a flower.
We don't want to do that forcibly.
It will happen, slowly.
Now, sit properly.
Your weight is balanced on the pin bones.
Your hands are on your lap.
You are cheerful and happy.
You are alert and vigilant.
Not sleepy.
In our heart we have the Lord and Guru.
The Lord protects us and Guru guides us from within.
We are nobody.
All the past knowledge regarding pranayama is kept aside.
Otherwise the mind will start comparisons, discussions etc..
Please do not have any plan about what you will do after meditation.
Now, in the present, we are going to practice fully and completely.
Never do anything half heartedly in life.
When we do anything half heartedly, we cannot grow spiritually,

Let Meditation Happen

in life.

Half heartedness is a very strong personality, because of constant evaluation and inability to let go.

We have to get into it fully, in the present, whole heartedly.

Now, you do it once. I have explained the sequence.

First breathe out.

Squeezing the stomach, inside upwards.

Then breathe in.

First in the stomach, then chest.

Breathe out, first from chest then stomach.

Again breathe in,

There is no hurry.

Don't count, but try to establish a rhythm of time taken for breathing in and breathing out as equal.

Go as deep in your breathing as well as full.

Very slow, no hurry.

After you do it, there are some observations to be noted.

1] Our breathing in and breathing out may not be equal. So, one has to consciously observe that a perfect rhythm is set.

2] Those who are doing it for the first time, for them to maintain the sequence of breathing in and out, may be difficult. But, don't worry. You will be able to achieve it with proper practice.

3] Not to hold the breath either inside or outside.

Now continue.

While we are breathing, slowly, deeply, remain fully aware of this process of breathing.

We must not be mechanical in practicing pranayama.

Don't concentrate on breathing but remain aware of it.

When you concentrate, breathing becomes important.

When you remain aware, the awareness is important.

You will notice that after a while, the asana has become firm on the base.

The body is vertically steady.

The weight of the body is distinctly felt on the pin bones.

Let Meditation Happen

The muscle tone in the muscles is minimum.
There may be one or two patches of tension, somewhere.
To give it a final touch,
get out of the body.
View the body from the front.
Go from the top to the bottom.
Part by part.
If there is any tension anywhere, relax it.

Now, see it from the right side and repeat the procedure -backside and left side.

Relax consciously.
Now, the body has become firm, steady and relaxed.
The body is now separated from the mind.
Hence, the concept of in or out of the body, does not hold good.

Because the shape, size and all the attributes of the body are dropped along with the body.

Our experience at this point is bodyless presence.
The breathing is extremely slow and shallow.
Remain aware that slow and shallow breathing is happening.
We are not doing it.

By persistent practice for long periods of time, one attains 'kevala kumbhaka'.

That is, neither holding the air, inside or outside, but letting the breathing stop totally.

Without efforts.
That is the ultimate in pranayama.
The moment you concentrate on breathing or body,
the thought process will begin, again.
So, be alert and vigilant.
Remain aware of shallow and slow respiration.
There will be almost negligible thought eruptions.

Now, during this process, when any thought comes, and we are not able to be indifferent, learn a very important lesson,

that whatever we have given importance to, positive or negative,

Let Meditation Happen

likes or dislikes, they are the source of this thought eruption.

Hence, every thought that comes in our mind,
reveals how many likes and dislikes we still have in our mind.
Initially, a lot of thoughts will come.
Get above that.
Thus, the mind will be emptied of its long stored disturbances.
We are perceiving all sounds very clearly.
We are not disturbed, because the mind is now like a mirror.
It is not a sleeping mind, like in deep sleep we don't hear anything.
Here, the mind is only reflecting the sounds and not reacting to the sounds.

Being free from body identification, this mind is now merged with the infinite mind, the total mind.

Hence, there cannot be any pressure anywhere in the body.
Eyes, between the eyebrows, head, there is no tension anywhere.
Like the space supports everything, but is not influenced by anything.

Be aware of the quality of breathing.
It will be slow and shallow.
Remain indifferent to all the things presented by the mind.
Slowly breathe deeper.
Move your toes and fingers.
Offer everything to the Lord.

✦✦✦

MEDITATION 8

We have to have a proper orientation when we do any job in our life.

For meditation our thoughts must be oriented towards divinity.

A method from 'Updesha saram' is to control speech.

So, we start with chanting.

Followed by the name of the Lord.

Then contemplation etc..

So, chant a stotra.

In the 'sadhana panchakam', there are 40 instructions about life.

The last instruction means, live as the infinite,

independent blissful conscious existence.

Do not live as a person in this relative world of achievements and failures.

Naturally, if this is the ultimate, then what else is required?

We have to think in terms of our own present identity.

We are extremely attached to the things and beings of this world.

We imagine that the world is going on because of our contribution.

We imagine that without us, the world will go nowhere.

As a result, under the disguise of so called responsibility,

we are more attached than responsible.

Our attachment to this world is glorified as responsibility

that we shoulder on our shoulders.

Therefore, Patanjali Maharshi says, the first important spiritual practice of 'yoga abhyas' is 'abhyas' and 'vairagya'.

Now, see how it helps.

When we have dispassion for worldly things, then our mind is free.

It is not occupied with the world.

What will happen to the mind that is not occupied with the world?

Naturally, that mind will now be absorbed towards its own source.

The more it goes towards its own source, the more there will

Let Meditation Happen

be detachment.

Less of attachment for the world.

In this manner, we have to start with 'vairagya'.

Dispassion.

This does not mean that we give up everything and start living under a tree.

In the 'Bhaja Govindam', it is said that the most important spiritual practice is to recognize that we are the victims of desire.

As long as any kind of desire is entertained in our mind, we are bound to suffer.

Once this understanding goes deeper and deeper, in all the activities of life, then meditation becomes great fun.

Our meditation is like 'sau chuhe khake billi haj pe chali'.

The whole day, we are terribly involved in this world, in a most disgusted, frustrated manner, and then we imagine, that once we sit for meditation, everything will be taken care of.

We are only cheating ourselves!

It will not happen.

Therefore, live a proper life of understanding, not a mechanical one.

Meditation has to be clearly defined in terms of goals and means.

The goal is that the gross body has to be dropped.

This gross body cannot be our correct identity.

With the gross body alone, the gross world begins.

With the gross body alone, good and bad, the whole relative gamut crops up.

Therefore, the first step is body disidentification.

Now, we have learnt a little about pranayama.

The purpose of pranayama is inner cleansing.

Just like we go to the toilet everyday, to get rid of the metabolic byproducts, which are in the form of solids.

Just like we have to urinate a few times a day, to get rid of the liquid unwanted wastes.

In the same manner, we have to clean our inner system of the toxic gases.

This is not a great deal. It is but a part of our daily lives.

So, this pranayama helps in removing the toxic gases and we do it two times a day, only for two minutes, with an empty stomach.

Slowly and steadily, over a period of time, the gaseous toxins will be removed from the body.

After this pranayama is done, we have to be aware that, is our attention again on our body?

That after this pranayama, I am feeling light.

Now I am feeling very enthusiastic.

Now I don't have a back pain.

These are all byproducts. They are not the purpose.

So, when we practice pranayama,

we should be very clear,

that the purpose is not anything else,

but, separating the body and mind from each other.

The mind and body are together, because of the prana.

Because of the breathing.

When breathing stops, mind and body are separated.

When the breathing is controlled, slowly, without going to sleep or dying,

there is a third possibility, living as embodied through the body, and not getting influenced by the modifications of the body etc..

This is the purpose of pranamaya kosha and its control.

If this holistic approach is not taken,

then what happens?

On the seat of meditation or pranayama, we will be doing everything very nicely, but all our attention will be on our health.

Not on reality.

Because, we see only what we have given importance to.

If health is important, we will forget the divine.

Therefore, people go to temples and ask the Lord for many things.

The purpose of our spiritual life is not this world.

How do we get out of it?

Let Meditation Happen

The most potent thing is understanding things correctly,
in the right perspective.
The body is bound to undergo change.
The body is bound to die one day.
Patanjali Maharshi says, 'aayu, jati, bhogah'
Where we are born,
what is the longevity of our life,
what are the experiences that we are going to go through?
It is predetermined.
Nobody can change that.
Then why worry about it?
If we are going to have diabetes, we will have it.
So, by proper education of the mind, we help separate the mind from the body.
After having achieved this, the second step is, who is the embodied?
Who is not the body. But before going into this, let us practice this once more.
Sit in such a manner, that the weight of the body is on the pin bones.
Do your legs still sleep after these few days of practice?
If they do not, then you have learnt properly.
If they do, it means that your posture is defective.
Do not sit at a 90 degree angle.
Reduce the angle a little, from the base itself.
Adjust the weight of the body, so that it lands exactly on the centre of gravity.
Keep your hands on your lap.
If your hands are on your knees, the hands start pulling you, after some time.
And the posture gets deflected.
Now, the basic psychological adjustments.
We have to repeat this everyday.
These are the basic errors with which we live throughout our lives.
First, remove the fear.

Let Meditation Happen

That is done by having faith that the Lord is seated in our heart, and the Guru is guiding us from within.

Second, we are practicing meditation by our own choice.

It is not compulsory and we are not obliging the world or God.

Do we feel proud that we have gone to the toilet?

Do we feel proud that we have taken a bath?

There is nothing to be proud about.

In the same manner, meditation is a daily involvement in the divine.

Third, we are Mr. Nobody.

Somebody is nothing but the summation of the total past.

With the load of the past, we cannot live happily in the present.

All thoughts start with us becoming somebody.

So, we remain as nobody as we were in deep sleep.

Then, we don't plan anything for after meditation.

By this, we block the future.

So, when the past and future are blocked, we are in the present.

Remaining in the present, we now practice pranayama.

Have the patience of a child, who is learning how to walk, when you do it.

It may not be perfect for the first few times.

So, we take a deep breath, slowly and fill our stomach fully.

Then we fill in our chest fully.

We don't hold the breath.

That will introduce pressure in our meditation.

We don't want to do anything under pressure.

So, after we have filled in our stomach and chest fully,
we slowly breathe out.

First from the chest, by collapsing the chest.

Then by squeezing the stomach inside upwards.

The air from the lower lobes of the lungs, is squeezed out.

Do it very slowly and deeply.

Today, we will learn the meaning of two terms.

Concentration and awareness.

Let Meditation Happen

When we practice pranayama, the first few times,
concentrate and see what happens.

When we concentrate, we go away from ourselves and into that in which we concentrate.

Therefore, concentration is in prakruti or matter.

Now just be aware that breathing is happening and you are an indifferent witness.

You will notice the difference.

When we remain aware of the breathing, it becomes slow and shallow.

It doesn't remain deep, anymore.

That is why Yagyavalka and Vashishtaji said, that the ultimate in pranayama is Kevala Kumbhaka.

In that state, we live more in awareness and so body disidentification happens.

When body disidentification happens, breathing is bound to be extremely slow and shallow.

Now you are breathing very slow and shallow.

This slow and shallow breathing is a gateway from matter to consciousness.

The mind loses the form and shape of the body,
hence the concept of inside and outside is no more valid.

Because, the mind has given up the shape of the body.

It is like, remaining like space and supporting the contents.

Space is common for all pots.

Pot space may appear to be different from each other,
but, in reality, every pot space is the same total space.

In the same manner, the mind appears to be separate for each person.

But, when body disidentification happens,
like the pot space when the pot is broken,
merges in total space, so does the mind merge in the total mind.

Remain as awareness.

Be yourself.

Let Meditation Happen

The formless, the beginningless, the endless... Therefore, like the waking comes and goes, the dream comes and goes, the deep sleep comes and goes, so is the story of Samadhi, meditation.

That also comes and goes.

This one consciousness, supporting all kinds of experiences, is ever the same.

We are not concentrating anywhere. Living as awareness.

Awareness does not need any medium of thoughts for establishing itself.

So, when we concentrate, we are riding the vehicle of thoughts and moving away to the object of concentration.

Awareness is thought free experience.

Concentration is a thoughtful experience.

When yoga is practiced unknowingly, we are only in matter. It is in fact not yoga.

When a seeker is no more concentrating on thoughts, whether thoughts are there or not, it makes no difference.

Then he is living in awareness.

That is the difference between concentration and awareness.

We can concentrate only on one thing at a time.

Because of the limitations of thoughts.

But, in awareness, one is able to be alert about everything around.

Living in awareness is living in spontaneity.

In concentration, there are efforts.

In awareness, there are no efforts.

As a result of efforts, we get tired, exhausted, fatigued. In awareness there are no efforts. Hence, no tiredness. Living in awareness, is living in meditation.

Meditation is no more a verb. Be alert and vigilant, lest we slip into concentration. Now, take a few deep breaths. Move your toes and fingers. Offer everything to the Lord. Don't carry any memory of the meditation or else it will become a concept. Truth is not a concept!

✦ ✦ ✦

MEDITATION 9

It is true that the mind can be quietened for some time, temporarily, by the application of the brake of pranayama.

But, this does not reduce the basic cause of disturbances in the mind.

If dirty clothes are piled up, folded and kept nicely.

From the surface level, it will seem that the clothes are very neatly packed and kept.

But, what is inside the clothes?

The same dirt, spots, smell, will be preserved deep within.

Now, when we unfold the clothes again, the dirt will still be there.

In the same manner, if you take a pain killer, it relieves but doesn't cure.

So, what is to be done?

What is the position of pranayama in meditation?

When we operate on something, that something must be under our control.

If we operate on a patient, the patient must be well secured.

So, how to secure the patient?

By wisdom?

Or by force?

Give him anesthesia, and he is controlled by force.

After that, operate on him.

You cannot give him anesthesia for six hours and then say, 'you will be alright'.

No.

So, pranayama is like keeping the mind under anesthesia, for a short period of time,

thereafter, we have to operate on the mind.

By the process of the 'laya', attained through pranayama, the mind becomes subtle.

Mind becomes quiet.

Let Meditation Happen

Then we have to destroy the mind.

The destruction of the mind is that, these habits that we have cultivated, in the mind,

regarding projection on every perception.

that has to be stopped.

If we want to understand the position of the mind,

let us imagine one example.

We stand in front of a mirror.

Suppose the mirror starts interacting with everything that is reflected in the mirror.

Suppose some good person comes, a beautiful girl comes,

the mirror will say, 'Oh please don't go. Hang on for sometime. I really like you.'

After that comes one old useless horrible fellow.

'Will you please get out!'

No.

The mirror only reflects.

Does not react. Does not interact.

Therefore, this mind has to go through two operations.

Operation 1- by the force of pranayama, make it shut up.

After that educate the mind.

Suppression accompanied by education leads to sublimation.

A sublimated mind alone, is a fit instrument for higher inquiry.

That is why, Bhagwan Raman Maharshi, told us this technique called 'veekshana pranayama' followed by 'ekchintanam'.

Reflecting on one thing, the mind is left with no option.

When there is zero option, the mind is on the threshold of its annihilation.

When we start giving more options to the mind, it becomes stronger and stronger.

When we give less options to the mind, it becomes weaker and weaker.

When we give no option to the mind, it is counting its last breaths.

Let Meditation Happen

So, let us now do the pranayama and start with the basic psychological adjustments.

We are here of our own choice.

We are cheerful and happy.

We have the Lord and Guru in our heart, who protect and guide us from within.

Third, we have to block our past once and for all.

To block the past, the simplest technique is, remain as Mr. Nobody.

So, on the seat of meditation, we are Mr. Nobody.

The total past is blocked.

We have no plans about what to do after meditation.

The future is blocked.

Now, in the present, we are sincere.

Not half hearted.

We start.

Breathe out, squeezing the stomach, inside upwards.

Then breathe in, very slowly, filling the stomach, then the chest.

Don't hold the breath.

Breathe out from the chest and then from the stomach.

Repeat it 8-10 times.

Try to set a perfect rhythm.

The time required for breathing in and out will be equal in due time.

Don't force.

So far we were concentrating on the breathing.

Now we continue the pranayama but become aware of the breathing process rather than concentrating.

A few observations.

Our base has become firm.

Vertically steady.

To a great extent the body is relaxed.

The weight of the body has increased on the pin bones.

The mind has given up the shape of the body.

Breathe normally.

Let Meditation Happen

Now, we will do the 'veekshana pranayama'.

So, let us understand the principle behind it.

One conscious existence expresses as the 'chitta' as well as the 'prana'.

Like we watch the movements of our own hands.

In the same manner, 'chitta' or the mind, is watching the breathing.

The knower and the known are expressions of the same.

When the mind becomes aware of the breathing,

the gap between the 'gyanshakti', mind, and the 'kriyashakti', prana, becomes minimum.

As a result, there will be hardly any thoughts in the mind.

The breathing will be almost suspended.

Neither inside nor outside.

This is 'kevala kumbhaka'.

Now we simply remain aware of the breathing, which is naturally going on.

Don't force anything on the breathing.

If you are forcing your concentration, or if you are forcing on the breathing,

you may get pressure or tension, in the head, eyeballs or the breathing may become erratic.

Don't force. Let it happen.

Now, recognize that breathing is not only happening through the nostrils but every cell of the body is breathing.

So, the whole body expands while breathing in and contracts while breathing out.

Now, observe this phenomenon.

Don't do anything.

The breathing will remain slow and shallow.

If you breathe deep, the mind will get tired and go to sleep.

Therefore, be alert.

Come to recognize that the in and out concept from the mind is removed.

Because, the body is dropped from the mind.

Let Meditation Happen

Now, in 'ekchintam', we are only aware of our own breathing.
When there is no other, the awareness is infinite.
There is only projection by the mind,
because the mind can project only on the objective perception.
Now we are nearly aware of our being not just a body or the embodied.
So, if the body is dropped, how can there be an embodied?
Do not watch the thoughts.
Remain aware of being.
When we watch thoughts, duality is maintained.
Like in the eyes.
We see anything else, vision is created.
But, when the eyes see themselves, vision disappears along with duality.
The mind is killed by reflecting on one.
That one which is absolute.
Absolute one is only infinite.
Mind can function only in the finite.
Like eyes can see the shapes and forms.
Formless cannot be seen by the eyes.
That is why space looks blue.
Our mind entertains many topics.
Now, only one topic.
That is, if we cannot be aware of our being, then one step lower, be aware of the silence, which is one.
Sounds are many.
Remaining aware of silence means, sounds although heard are not reacted with.
Don't concentrate on any part of the body.
Awareness is not inside or outside the body.
Like the snake on the rope is not inside the rope, nor outside the rope.
In the same manner, awareness alone is the truth.
In this awareness, the illusion of the body, and the embodied,

create a sense of inside for the body and outside about the world.
When you are disturbed because of too many thoughts,
don't suppress them.
But notice who is having the thoughts.
So, the father, mother, brother, they have the thoughts.
We have already taken the position of nobody.
Now, can there be any thoughts?
Therefore, thought presence clearly tells, that Mr. Nobody has become Somebody.

In awareness, there is nobody.
Hence, there are no thoughts.
In deep sleep there is nobody.
But there is no recognition of awareness.
It is utter ignorance.
Hence, sleep can be repeated.
Awareness cannot. It is ever the same.

The moment you become aware about the thought process, whatsoever important it may be, in the presence of awareness, thought disappears.

The moment there is inadvertence, 'pramad', old habits take over.
Remain alert. Vigilant. And quiet.

Now as you will start breathing deeper, slowly, you can clearly experience how the body shape is regained in the mind. The concept of inside and outside has become valid. The world of relativity from one to many has emerged. Mind becomes vibrant, functioning in relativity.

✦✦✦

MEDITATION 10

An ignorant observation means an observation made by an ignorant person.
Like we have elementary physics.
Physics is not elementary.
It is meant for elementary students.
Similarly, ignorant observation tells us,
that when breathing stops, life stops.
Breathing or prana is the atma or soul.
When prana goes out, and doesn't come back,
we consider that life is only because of the prana.
Katha Upanishad does not agree.
It says, living beings do not live because of breathing.
They are alive because of something else.
The breathing is also dependent on this something else.
It is not because of breathing that we are alive.
It is because of some factor, because of which breathing is possible.
And therefore, life is possible.
So, this statement of the Upanishad asks us to rethink our understanding about breathing.
So, when we are alive, we breathe.
Therefore, we can control the prana.
That which is controlled is different from the controller.
The controller is not dependent on the controlled.
The controller is independent for its existence.
Like a car can be controlled, and the owner of the car is the controller.
So, movement of the car is because of the owner, not because of the car.
In the same manner, this prana, the vital air, its going and coming, is dependent on some other factor.
Therefore, when the breathing is going on heavily or slowly, or it

is stopped forcibly by Rechak kumbhaka or pooraka kumbhaka, all this is possible only because there is something which is controlling it.

This is to be inquired into.

Therefore, we are working on the pranamaya kosha.

First it was the annamaya kosha.

Now it is the pranamaya kosha.

Then we will work on the manomaya, vijnayanamaya and anandamaya koshas.

When we are sitting and controlling prana, this is what will help us change our wrong notions and help in correct understanding.

When we are breathing in, we know that the air has gone in.

When we do the pooraka kumbhaka, hold the air inside, the prana is also inert.

It is held by the will of someone other than the prana.

Then we breathe out.

This is also a controllable thing.

We can breathe out fast or slow.

Therefore, our identity is certainly not prana.

It is only the means.

This prana is possible because of this conscious existence which is expressing in the body.

as a movement, spanda, throb.

When consciousness does not have a throb, that baby is considered to be still born.

The baby is born, but it has no life.

So, what is lacking?

From a living mother, how can a dead baby come?

Then what has happened?

The consciousness which is very much present in the body has not been initiated into a throb.

For whatever reason.

When the baby's body is exposed to a sudden change in temperature, immediately there is some kind of jerk that the consciousness within the body gets, because of which the throb begins.

Once this happens, then breathing is a continuous process.

Because of this throb of consciousness, the diaphragm becomes flat.

When it becomes flat, air is sucked in.

Again the diaphragm becomes normal position, so the convexity of the diaphragm, presses against the lungs, and air is breathed out.

In this manner, breathing is initiated and continues.

This breathing indicates the throb of consciousness called life.

So, there are 2 things.

One is consciousness.

Second is throb of consciousness of life.

The expression of life is breathing.

Because of the breathing and the movements of consciousness, this moving consciousness, as if throws waves of thoughts and waves of thoughts create another phenomena called mind, which results into I versus you, as one expression of the mind, and inner controller of life as another.

So, mind as inner controller is the common undivided substratum which is controlling the expression of life.

So, blood circulation, digestion, excretion, metabolism, it all goes on.

The second aspect of the mind is that mind has been influenced by the shape and form of the body.

Because of that, the mind thinks only with reference to that particular body.

This is how an individuality is born.

So, when we practice pranayama, what is achieved is, only this, that slowly slowly, the mind remains only as inner controller and shape and form of the body disappear from the mind.

When the mind is liberated from the shape and form of the body, as it merges in the infinite mind where differences have no place.

That is one of the most important observations.

If our practice is for knowing the truth, self realization, then we must not allow the mind to take the shape of the body.

Let Meditation Happen

As the mind drops the body shape, the breathing automatically becomes slow and shallow.

Now, we have been in the field of matter, up to now.

The 'veekshana pranayama' that Bhagwan Raman Maharshi spoke about, is,

we remain aware of this whole process.

If the breathing was irregular, it was when the mind was fully attached to the body.

When sense of duality, the world, otherness, limited existence, were real.

When the breathing is slow and shallow, in both these conditions, this presence or consciousness does not have any influence.

Recognition of this unchanging conscious principle is living in meditation.

Now, if you observe or recognize how the body is seated,

the asana has become firm at the base.

The body is vertically steady.

The weight of the body is slowly increasing and felt on the pin bones.

The form of the body is slowly disappearing from the mind.

The breathing without any special effort is extremely slow and shallow.

Efforts are only in the finite.

In the infinite, efforts are not.

The complete picture is that the body is seated without movement, fully relaxed, breathing is slow and shallow.

The shape of the body is on the verge of disappearance from the mind.

Therefore, the mind merges in the infinite.

Because of old habits, when any perception happens,

the mind reacts or meaningless thoughts keep on appearing.

But, we are not giving any importance to that.

Now, we are no more bothered about the body, the world, prana, etc..

Let Meditation Happen

Remain alert.

Do not suck yourself inside, or else suppression is developed in the head.

All abnormalities start manifesting.

No.

We are not interested in the light of the bulb.

We are interested in the electrical energy.

This energy doesn't have any shape or form, any functional goal.

In the same manner, this conscious existence is infinite.

If the mind thinks, it always thinks about something which has a shape or a name.

Hence, to free the mind from shape, we break the barrier of our body shape and merge the mind in space.

Space is formless. The mind also becomes formless.

The formless, shapeless mind is consciousness.

When the mind takes a position that there is absence of forms and shapes, of waking and dreaming,

this position of mind, absent of shapes and forms, as an object creates deep sleep.

It is not merging the mind in the shapeless reality.

Because the mind is still functioning in the relative realm.

In waking and dream the object was name and form.

In the deep sleep, objective, no name, no form.

So, absence has become formless.

We are not talking about absence.

We are talking about presence.

Waking has come and gone.

Presence is untouched.

So with the other realms and experiences.

In other words,

the clouds of waking, dream, etc

they appear in this conscious space for some time and then disappear.

The conscious space is not influenced by this.

MEDITATION 11

The intensity of breathing is responsible for our identification with mind and body.

So, mind and body, remain together with the same intensity, as our breathing.

We all have seen and known, that when breathing stops, there is the death of the body.

Therefore, there is this fear, when the breathing is extremely slow and shallow, one develops an unknown fear and we breathe heavily again,

resulting in body identification.

Therefore, the first thing is to be fully convinced.

Katha Upanishad says, 'not by the prana or apana are we alive'.

Because we are alive, we are breathing.

It is the other way round.

The controller of breathing cannot be breathing.

The controller of the car is not the car.

So, without this clear understanding,

that our identity is not either with the body or with the breathing.

It is for this purpose, that pranayama is practiced.

When we practice pranayama, slowly, nadi shodhanam takes place.

The mind starts disowning the shape of the body.

As mind starts disowning shape and size of the body, the body starts becoming heavier and the muscle tone is reduced to the minimum.

Because, now the mind is slowly disowning the shape of the body.

So, now, only one aspect of the mind is functioning.

The inner controller.

Because of which the body metabolism continues, life continues to exist.

Hence, we do the pranayama with this understanding.

Every time you sit for meditation, convince yourself that body

Let Meditation Happen

dis identification is the goal.

When this becomes clear, we will not develop pressure in our cranium, or give importance to anything that is happening with the body.

Now, practice pranayama for 5 minutes.

Observe the breathing from being outside the body.

Breathe slowly.

Take the front view of the body and relax if there are any patches of tension.

If you are not fully dis identified, then you will be struggling to take the front view of your body or any other view.

Because you are still holding yourself inside the body.

If this is the case, start from the beginning.

Relax the head, forehead, eyebrows, eyeballs, nose, lips, chin, face, ears.

Relax relax relax.

The neck from the front side and back side, the shoulders,
relax the upper arms, elbows, lower arms, wrist, palm and fingers.

Relax the main trunk, chest, sides, upper back, abdomen and below, sides up to the hip joints, from upper back downwards slowly go up to the pin bones.

Relax the hips, thighs, knees, calves, ankles, heels and toes.

Like so many bodies, there is one body which we claim to be ourselves and ours.

But, now we have dropped the body.

In fact, body relaxation means body dis identification.

Now, if we are fully dis identified, do the same experiment where we left off.

Take the front view of the body, remaining outside.

You can clearly see the difference in the experiment.

Now, we are able to objectively view the head, forehead etc., not from inside but from outside.

Recognize this difference.

Now view the right side.

Let Meditation Happen

Now you are not struggling to remain inside.

Because body dis identification has happened to a great extent.

Go to the backside of the body and take the view.

Then take the left view.

Now there is no doubt whatsoever, that our identity is the embodied and not the body.

It is like the pot space has come out of the pot and started looking at the pot from outside.

And it has come to recognize that the pot space is not limited by the pot walls.

Thus, the pot space comes to recognize itself to be the infinite space.

In the same manner, the concept of inside and outside the body is gone. Because the shape and figure of the body is ironed out.

Now it is only the presence where perception of sounds is heard.

But, it is no more disturbing.

The mind is like a mirror.

It reflects everything.

It doesn't get influenced or make impressions on its surface.

When the body shape disappears from the mind, the world of forms also disappears.

Now, our experience is formless existence.

Hence, awareness about the sounds is there, but the sounds don't influence.

Similarly, let us remain aware of the silence.

The next hurdle is our habitual thinking.

Now the world is not disturbing.

Sounds and silence are the same.

The forms disappear.

Now, the old habit of habitual thinking comes in.

Now, be aware that thoughts only come when you become somebody.

When we become somebody, thoughts are in relation to that personality.

Let Meditation Happen

Now, drop this identity as Somebody, and remain as Nobody.
This nobody is nothing other than awareness.
Hence, no thoughts.
So, today we have seen how complete relaxation of the body leads to dis identification.
We can observe our body from outside the body.
It was this that Bhagwan Raman Maharshi did, when someone had died.
He simply came, lied down on the bed, and could clearly experience that his identity was not the body.
In the same manner, we come to this conviction, that body dis identification means remaining as nobody, and nobody is awareness, and that in awareness there are no thoughts.
Therefore, living as awareness is living in meditation.
Not doing meditation.
Because meditation is an experience between the absolute and the relative.
By regular long experience of this meditation, the earlier notion that we are the body, weakens.
That we are the embodied, becomes clear.
Then alone is the next step possible, as to who is this embodied.
Hence the goal of meditation initially is body dis identification without going to sleep or death.
Now you can very clearly experience that the body had nothing to do with our existence.
This eternal presence, independent of the body is the truth.
Now, breathe deeper slowly.
Don't do anything forcibly.
Don't take any jerks.
Slowly let the bud open.
Now take one two deep breaths.
Move your toes and fingers.
Offer everything to the Lord.
Come to realize how body identification is complete.

MEDITATION 12

Metabolic processes of the body are maintained by the mind without formation of thoughts. But, when the mind takes the shape of the body, that aspect of mind is responsible for formation of thoughts.

It is on this vehicle of thoughts, that we go away from our own selves.

This going away from our own selves happens in 3 parameters.

Time

Space

Object.

Therefore, one of the essential ingredient of controlling the mind is engaging the mind with reference to these three parameters.

When we control the mind, we simply suppress it by the force of pranayama. The moment the brake of pranayama is lifted, the mind starts running with double speed. We will try to learn how we can control the mind by engaging the mind with reference to these three parameters.

First we take the grossest among the three. That is object. Our mind runs from one object to another. If the mind has discovered real fulfillment in a particular object, then it should not run from one place to another. But, this does not happen.

The mind does not find fulfillment in any object.

Therefore, the mind tries to obtain one object.

Then, after some time, goes in search of another object.

This is how the mind makes a fool of us.

Therefore, we have to give some object to the mind, so that it does not run, here and there. Secondly, that which we love the most, for that our mind runs again and again.

Therefore, for controlling the mind, an ingredient of love is required. That is why we have some God or Guru as an alter of worship and we engage our mind with reference to this object.

Let Meditation Happen

Suppose we are the devotees of Bhagwan Shri Krishna, then, the Lord alone is given prime importance in our thinking process.

The second parameter is place. This is subtler than object.

So, we feel the presence of the Lord, in one place.

Not everywhere. That one place, may be our heart.

Not the bloody one.

The one in the sternum, in the middle of the chest, where the ribs join.

It is only here that the consciousness manifests for the first time.

It is only here that the mind begins after the throb.

So, the sternum, where the diaphragm is attached, that is our spiritual heart. So, we bring our mind, without much effort to this sternum point. It has become the place.

Object is the Lord.

So, object and place are dealt with.

Third thing is time.

So, we engage our mind with reference to one object, one place for a long time. So, here there are two types of practices.

1] Sound base
2] form base

Because, 'nama rupa', name and form are the problem. So, today we take the name. Now our mind is fixed in the spiritual heart on the conscious form of Bhagwan Shri Krishna.

We take the support of chanting the Lords name. In the 'upadesha saram', are given four stages of speech. You may chant in your mind or loudly.

This will keep the mind engaged. The mind engaged for one job for a long period of time is called Samadhi. Samprajnat yoga.

There is no hurry. Pronounce each and every letter slowly and in our heart. So, the name of the Lord begins from the heart, remains there and concludes there only. Let us chant 'Hari Om', ten times. In this chanting process, importance is given to the name. Each mantra is chanted slowly without any pressure of any kind.

Then we leave some gap, and in that gap, there are no other

thoughts intercepting.

Then chant again.

In this practice, the observation that we have to make with reference to engaging the mind, is that we chant a series of names, without any dissimilar thought coming in between.

So let us chant once again keeping all these instructions in mind.
Hari Om
18-20 times.

This is one aspect of the engagement of the mind.

What we do is, chant three times, continuously and then stop for some time.

Again chant three times, again silence.

Silence is maintained till any other thought is absent,
and when we feel that some thought is likely to come,
again we chant.

Thus, dissimilar thoughts are not allowed to enter the mind.

Then we increase the number from three to five.

Increase the gap between the two chantings.

Here also, the same observation. No dissimilar thoughts come in between.

With long practice we can chant the Lords name, without any dissimilar thoughts coming in between.

This ability to be engaged in the same purpose, for a long period of time, is called Samadhi.

So, let us chant once more.

This time our attention should be on silence rather than sounds.

In that we have to recognize that silence is eternal.

Sounds have a beginning and end.

We remain with the silence.

Hear the sounds as well as silence.

See how words are just a disturbance in silence.

Hari Om
5 times.

Keep the attention on the silence.

Let Meditation Happen

Hari Om
5 times.
When a seeker practices this for a few years,
the world loses its potency.
The mind remains undisturbed although perception continues.
In other words, the mind becomes like a mirror.
Now. Practice for some time. Extend the silence zone.
You must have observed that it is easier for the mind to go on chanting, but then, it becomes mechanical.
We are not interested in that.
We want to engage the mind as per our decision.
Hence, when we chant three times, the mind must observe silence.
Try again. So, our conclusion is, words come and go. Silence is uncreated, neither comes, nor goes. In silence, words are disturbances.
In the same manner, thoughts are disturbances in the mind.
Thoughts are born, they remain for some time, they disappear.
With many words, sentences are formed.
With many thoughts, mind is formed.
With sentences of words, world is created.
With thoughts together, ego is created.
Hence, lesser words mean lesser world.
Lesser thoughts. Lesser ego.
Ultimately, no thoughts, no ego.
Thought free mind is consciousness.
Even when there are thoughts, mind is consciousness.
But thoughts become so overpowering that it seems as though consciousness is covered by a sheet of thoughts. On this substratum of the non dual consciousness, because of the importance of thoughts, the world of relativity appears. Hence, the importance of controlling the mind.
Breathe slowly, deeper. Move your fingers and toes. Offer everything to the Lord. Don't make a memory of the experience.

✦ ✦ ✦

Let Meditation Happen

MEDITATION 13

The mind has two aspects.

1] Aspect of perception: If the mind is not associated in interaction such as, our eyes are open and our mind is somewhere else.

In that condition, a person or object is in front of us, but we don't recognize the presence of that object or person.

Therefore, this is the perceptive aspect of the mind.

Unless something is perceived, there cannot be interaction.

Interaction is also of two types.

a. We like that object.

b. We dislike that object.

Liking and disliking objects is without any logic, without any reason.

It is just like that.

And our whole life is based on our likes and dislikes.

Therefore, we have to consciously work on this.

That, are we functioning under the influence of likes and dislikes?

Or, are we functioning under the influence of wisdom?

For that, we must know the working of the mind.

When the mind works with something,

interacts with somebody,

if liking is an interaction, there will be a kind of dent in the mind, of liking.

If there is something that we don't like, then there will be another dent of disliking.

The mind carries only these two categories of interaction.

It doesn't matter, whether the liking is for a person, place, food, fragrance, just anything.

All of them deposit their impressions of liking in one channel.

Similarly, the disliking for any person, place etc. is deposited in another channel.

Initially, the mind carries these channels and later they become

grooves.
Then they become valleys as they increase.
Likes and dislikes become extremely prominent and strong.
As we move on a road, if the road is plain and smooth, no problem.
But, if there are speed breakers at every little distance, then we get unnecessarily jerked.
Our mind is like riding on a road, with only speed breakers.
Therefore, our 'sadhana' is to work on leveling these speed breakers of likes and dislikes.
The first 'sadhana', is discipline.
We do not like many things. But if they are right, they should be done.
Then only can we go beyond likes or dislikes.
We used to have a rule in our house.
Whatever is given in the plate for eating, should be eaten.
There was never a question of liking or disliking any food.
Nobody used to ask, 'Would you like to have this?'
No. Eat this. Over.
Now, what is the net result?
Net result is, food is no problem, throughout the world.
Very often, food becomes a major problem.
'Unless I get this or that, I cannot survive.'
These kind of likes and dislikes can be overcome only by discipline.
Secondly, we have to force ourselves to come out of these likes and dislikes.
This forcible implementation of the principle must be followed by education of the mind.
First suppression. Then education.
This leads to sublimation.
In this manner, the mind slowly becomes cultured.
Our mind is a wild one, now.
A garden is not any place where trees and plants grow.
That is a jungle.

Let Meditation Happen

A garden is where selected plants are allowed to grow.
That too in discipline and unwanted weeds are removed.
In the same manner, only because there are thoughts in the mind, it is not cultured or thoughtful.
We have to weed out the unwanted thoughts.
Only the required thoughts should remain.
We have to look after our mind as a gardener looks after his garden.
With great love.
Every delicate plant is given attention.
All unwanted grass and weeds are taken out.
When we are working with the mind, in this manner, we will succeed in erasing likes and dislikes.
Bhagwan says in the Gita, 'The purpose of Karma is not to improve the world. The purpose of Karma is to be able to clean our mind.'
Our mind is carrying the load of personal likes and dislikes.
Unless personal likes and dislikes are cleaned, we are not walking the spiritual path.
It is necessary to understand all this.
After this is done, the second aspect of the mind can be worked upon, on the seat of meditation.
If you study the anatomy of any thought, you will see,
mind plus the value that we give to anything or anybody, together constitute a thought.
Mind plus any value, positive or negative, is a thought.
When we think about our home.
we have given a positive value to our home,
Therefore, the home thought is born.
If we don't have a home, home thought cannot come.
Thought is the value that we give to anything in this world.
So, if the award of value is an entry permit for that object in our mind,
thereby creating a thought,

what will be the way, to quieten the thought formation?

If we have given value to something or somebody, we have to devalue it.

That devaluation is done through wisdom and understanding.

Like, we give value to a particular thing.

If that particular thing happens the way we want, we will be happy.

If it doesn't happen, we will be miserable.

So, if I am wise enough, I will work on the mind.

'Look here, I have given importance to this, because of which the mind is getting disturbed.'

Now the question raised is, 'Is it worth losing our peace of mind for anything or anybody in the whole world?'

It is not worth it.

Because, if we put the peace of mind on one side of the scale, and the whole world on the other side of the scale,

the peace of mind is more important than anything else.

With this educating technique, we work on the mind.

So, when we are sitting quiet, various thoughts are bound to come.

We identify ourselves with those thoughts.

eg: when identification takes place with the thought of the daughter, a father or mother is born. Then thoughts come in great speed, one after another.

So, we have to be ruthless right in the beginning.

'I am Mr. Nobody.'

No father, no mother.

So, for some time there will be freedom from thoughts.

Then, another thing enters the mind. Again you have to stop.

You have to be firm with yourself on the seat of meditation.

In this manner, consciously, with great vigilance and alertness, one has to practice indifference, through education of the mind.

Secondly, it is not that we get thoughts only when we have become somebody or given importance to something.

Unknown thoughts rise up in the mind, too.

Let Meditation Happen

By chanting the Lord's name and controlling thoughts is one method of doing it.

Today let us practice indifference.

Neither suppression nor appreciation of thoughts.

The mind is something like a spoilt child.

It wants constant attention.

To seek attention, like the child climbs on the body and holds the face of the mother, with its tiny hands, and draws attention physically.

In the same manner, the mind does the same thing.

If we give importance to such a child, it will soon climb on top of our head.

If you scold him, he will make a mess.

The only way to be with him is remain indifferent.

So, never fight with the mind.

Learn to remain indifferent.

What happens when we remain indifferent?

Please understand this.

When we give attention to any thought,
that thought gathers reality and existence.

The thought becomes real when we give attention to it.

Then the mind feeds on the apparently real thought.

In this manner, there is mutual dependence.

Thoughts gather existence from us and the I thought feeds on these objective thoughts and becomes stronger and fatter.

So, when we remain indifferent to thoughts,
thoughts become weak and automatically die away.

When there is starvation for the I thought, because there is no objective thought to feed on, the thought aspect of I thought is dropped.

Only thought free experience remains.

Now, this is the principle.

Play with this principle.

Become brother, sister, father, mother, and see how thoughts

related to them come up.
Remain with those thoughts for a few moments.
Now start.
See the clear picture when identified with one individuality as mother, father etc..
There was a momentum in the thinking process.
The moment this is dropped, the momentum stops.
Thought free experience remains.
All sounds are heard, but, now the mind is like a mirror.
No classification.
No reaction.
So, the perceptive aspect of the mind, does not create any bondage.
The projection aspect creates the problem.
When we are over projecting by habit,
we don't perceive what is.
We perceive our own minds projection.
When we were chanting the Lords name,
there were some efforts.
We remain indifferent.
Like space is indifferent to all that is happening in space.
Instead of participating in the theme, we remain aware that unwanted thoughts are rising.
The moment we become aware, do not join with the thoughts.
They die away.
If you recognize these thoughts,
they are either memories or worries of the past or future.
In the absolute present, there cannot be any thought.
Therefore, on the vehicle of these thoughts,
we go away from our own conscious blissful self.
Now breathe deeper.
Move your toes and fingers.
Offer everything to the Lord.

✢ ✢ ✢

MEDITATION 14

We are working on the mind.
Working on the mind means working in three areas.
a. Reduction in frequency of thoughts per second
b. Changing the direction of thoughts
c. Improving the quality of thoughts.

For this purpose, the quality of thoughts depend upon the object entertained by the thought.

The most dear in the whole world is the paramatma.

This is the supreme reality.

Therefore, when our mind is entertaining divine thoughts, our mind is pure.

When the mind is entertaining worldly thoughts, our mind is impure.

This impurity will keep bothering us throughout life.

Therefore,
a. Divine must be the theme in the mind.
b. Reducing the quantity of thoughts per second. There are many thoughts which are constantly erupting in the mind. So, first of all, reduce the variety of thoughts. This can be done by holding onto one thought. That one thought could be the Lords name or the mantra which we use for chanting. So, we continue with this one thought. So that there is not too much work for the mind. Reduce thoughts to zero. It is not possible in one go. Therefore we take only one name of the Lord.

Om Namah Shivaya
Three times.

What happens is, the mind entertains the divine theme, and variety of thoughts are reduced.

When we chant continuously, thoughts are many, but they are of the same species. Divine.

Let Meditation Happen

When thoughts are of the same species, although they are many, that does not make much difference.

That is the importance of 'japa sadhana'.

So, we have made the thoughts pure.

Qualitative and quantitative improvement.

Patanjali Maharshi says that the mind flows in two directions.

A river flows only in one direction, but the river of the mind flows in two directions.

Towards the world objectively and towards the self subjectively.

Objective flow of the mind is known to us and is convenient.

That has been our training throughout life.

What can we do?

We keep this objective flow intact, but instead of thinking about worldly things,

we make God as the altar of our thought.

And we continue with the duality.

So, devotion begins objectively with duality, but the mind is now changing the direction.

It is not going the world way, but it is going the God way.

When this is consciously practiced, we will slowly reduce the frequency of thoughts,

changing the quality of thoughts and changing the flow of thoughts from world to God.

What Patanjali Maharshi says is, thoughts can be ultimately suspended from formation by 'abhyasa', practice.

Therefore, when we are chanting the Lords name, first our attention is that we are culling the variety of thoughts, and reducing them to one thought.

Om Namah Shivaya

Three times.

Now, in this practice, see that no dissimilar thought enters in the garland of your mantra chanting.

Now, repeat this mantra in your mind.

Om Namah Shivaya

Let Meditation Happen

Nine times.
Chant each mantra consciously. Not mechanically.
Let there be a wider gap between two chantings.
Where there are no thoughts, in this gap.
When you feel a thought is likely to erupt, chant again.
Om Namah Shivaya
Three times.
You must have observed,

there is a tendency, when the chanting synchronizes with the breathing.

If this is encouraged, chanting becomes mechanical.

We don't want to do that.

Hence, be careful that breathing and chanting don't establish a rhythm.

Our goal is to go beyond the presence and absence of thoughts.

Now, chanting begins, remains and terminates.

But, conscious presence, neither has a beginning, middle or end.

This is our essential nature.

When there are thoughts, nothing is added to the mind.

When thoughts are not there, there is no loss.

This clear cut discrimination between 'purusha', the consciousness, and 'prakruti', thoughts, is called 'viveka khyati'.

The vigilance has to be that other than the mantra, no thought is entertained.

This alertness is 'viveka khyati'.

If we are not vigilant, old habits, worldly thoughts, will overtake chanting of the Lords name.

Breathe deeper.

Move your toes and fingers.

Offer everything to the Lord.

✦ ✦ ✦

MEDITATION 15

The body does not think.
The prana does not think.
The worldly objects do not think.
Therefore, they are happy.
They are not miserable.
Our mind also does not have the capacity to think, independent of the light of consciousness.
Therefore, mind is also inert.
It is the Absolute Reality that has its inherent potentiality, call it maya, prakruti, avyakta, etc..
There being nothing to act upon, this maya or prakruti, will like to act upon the absolute reality, to which it belongs.
Suppose I have a potentiality for singing.
When I become aware of my potentiality, what will happen?
I will like to sing.
Now, this potentiality of singing cannot be invoked in anybody other than me, because it is my potentiality.
Now, in me, there being none other than me, whom will it effect?
It will only effect me.
So, the potentiality will not sing.
The potentiality will make me sing.
Then, instead of me remaining as a human being, I will become a singer.
When I become a singer, I will like to sing.
Subsequently, I will want to recognize myself as a singer of the millennium.
And the whole life is now bound on that one potentiality.
Therefore, instead of remaining as a human being, I will become a singer.
So, remaining human being is Brahman.
Becoming a singer is a jiva.

Let Meditation Happen

Now, who can help me to get out of this limitation of singing?
Only I have to recognize that.
That I am not only a singer.
There are many more things.

In the same manner, parabrahma with this infinite potentiality, will create its impact on itself as maya or prakruti.

This maya will not influence the parabrahma.
Like sweetness cannot influence sugar,
Heat cannot influence fire,
So also this infinite potentiality will not influence parabrahma.
Then there will be an illusion that this infinite potentiality has influenced the parabrahma.

It will seem as if it is influencing, but in fact it is not.
This is how the jiva is born.
We play with this idea, when we sit for meditation.
We will not struggle.
Keep the mind shut down.
It will not happen this way.
For ultimate understanding, 'viveka khyati' is required.
That cannot happen without enquiry,
without reflection,
without mananam.

For making ourselves capable of this reflection, leading to mananam and discrimination, clearly, we are on the seat of meditation.

Now, I will introduce one more new topic.
There is a lot of emphasis given on the 'asana siddhi'.
One must attain perfection in asana.
Let us understand the secret behind this.

The mind is disturbed because of its inability to cope with different situations.

Likes and dislikes are overpowering.
We have to overcome the overpowering effects of likes and dislikes.
This capacity of endurance and rising above personal likes and dislikes,

is attained by 'asana siddhi', by the perfect asana.

So, we sit in a proper posture and refuse to move.

You must have experienced that when we sit,

the mind gives us suggestions.

Scratch here, move this part of the body, etc..

These are the tricks of the mind,

because the moment the body starts becoming stabilized, mind is approaching its death.

When the body is firm, steady and fully relaxed,

mind is giving up the shape of the body,

that is the death of the mind.

Therefore, the mind suggests that there is pain somewhere,

there is scratching somewhere.

So that, we get identified with the body again and the mind survives.

Hence, perfection in asana increases our ability to face adversities without complaint and without difficulty.

Now, in this analysis, although we are practicing asana,

our attention is on the mind.

That the mind must be liberated from the two valleys of likes and dislikes.

It is for this purpose that we practice 'sthira sukham asanam'.

Now the mind has become sufficiently steady.

The tamoguna, laziness, sleepiness, has gone and the body is parked on the seat.

So the pramad, habitual identification with the body is also given up to a great extent.

Now the second aspect.

This quietness of the mind is not the goal.

The goal is 'viveka khyati'.

The five objects keep the eleven senses preoccupied and they are mutually dependent.

But the purusha tattva, is absolutely independent.

It being one without a second.

Let Meditation Happen

Then, the 'asmita', the I ness, and the pancha tanmatra, that is the first division in the mahattattva, means dichotomization of the consciousness into subjective objective phenomena.

I ness versus not I ness.

This is the first division.

This consciousness, mahattattva, is nothing but absolute existence.

In this process of viveka khyati, discrimination between purusha tattva and prakruti and its modification, one has to remain aware that thoughts are constantly coming and going.

That thought which is given importance to, lingers.

When we no more give importance to that thought, it disappears.

Thereby, we have to learn that we have to devalue every theme in the whole universe.

Make it clear in your understanding, that whatever we give importance or value to, that is a cause of thought formation and maintenance.

If we have given importance to something, we have to drop it.

Now, see the mind is sufficiently quiet.

With lots of thoughts, body identification becomes obvious.

It is difficult to quieten the mind, at this stage, as you are.

Relax the body.

The pressure which has developed inside the body, will drop.

The mind will merge with the infinite.

Now see the difference.

Every relative thought strengthens body identification.

Hence, whenever thoughts are becoming too many, without changing anything, just relax the body.

Like the deflation of a tyre or a balloon, the body will be dropped from the mind.

✦ ✦ ✦

MEDITATION 16

The mind is recognized as an interaction between two types of thoughts, the I thought and the not I thought.

Normally, we get carried away by the theme of the thoughts we are entertaining. And we go away from ourselves either in time, in space or in objects. Some thoughts pertaining to the distant past, distant places, different objects, for all these, we get identified with them and this pure I, the absolute conscious self, because of the identification with these objective thoughts, becomes a relative subject.

This absolute self is reduced to relative subject by identifying with those objective thoughts and being subject clothed in thoughts, is called as a subjective thought. Thus, in the pure object, there is no samsara. In pure subject, there is no samsara. But, when the object, time, place etc. are included in the mind, and the subject is also included in the mind, because of the conditioning of the mind, the subjective and objective thoughts result.

Relativity or samsara is for these thoughts. Hence, yoga talks about,' yogah chitta vritti nirodah'. This means that these thoughts with the object as the content, they are frozen. The contents of the thoughts are aborted by viveka khyati, by discrimination between purusha and prakruti. When the objective thoughts abort objects, the contentless thought is pure mind.

Now, what happens to the subjective thought?

When the subjective thought does not have objective thoughts to feed upon, the thought aspect of the subject, disappears. Thereafter, objectless, thoughtless or thought free subject is left behind. This objectless awareness and thought free I, together constitute the absolute conscious self. Hence, the practice will be to remain indifferent to the world.

Now, sit quietly.

Stabilize the perfect posture. When the posture is perfect, base firm, steady and fully relaxed, the mind has dropped the body shape, which creates individuality.

Now, the next step is, just be indifferent to every thought that erupts. Take a position of space and as space remains undisturbed by what it supports, in the same manner, remain as solid space.

Solid space means no contents.

The solidness is not a void, it is a presence.

This conscious solid space is one without a second.

Like deep waters have no waves.

Waves start appearing at the surface.

In the same manner, in the depth of consciousness, there are no thoughts, no mind.

Do not pull yourself inside.

Do not concentrate on any place, object, merely remain aware.

When we concentrate, mind is created.

Therefore, don't concentrate.

When the thought process sets in mechanically, we do not even become aware of that.

But, become identified with the thought process, and thinking becomes intense.

Rather than dropping the mind, we strengthen the existence of the mind.

To avoid this, remain aware of the quality of breathing.

Breathing must be slow and shallow.

When the breathing quality is monitored, the thought process does not begin.

Don't concentrate on the breathing or body.

Remain aware of being. Take a deep breath. When this body shape comes in the mind, again, the body starts appearing real, world is created and mind starts operating.

This transmission from consciousness to the mind when it is clearly recognized, one can halt it any moment. Thereby the 'drasta' and 'drushya' are distinct.

✦ ✦ ✦

MEDITATION 17

Bhagwan Shankaracharya tells us in 'sadachar', that when we know something objectively, there are two stages.
a. This is an object
b. I know this is an object.

So, there is the objective aspect of the thought and subjective aspect of the thought. Whenever there is objectivity in knowledge, it is finite. Mind can function only in the kingdom of finite. Finites are many. This is how the mind survives. With every object known, a fresh knower is born. Thus, if many objects are known, over a long period of time, many knowers are born.

They are put together in the string of consciousness and an ego is born. Therefore, 'I have gone there, I know this, I know that'.

Now, if the number of objects known is less, to that extent, number of knowers will be less.

Like for a child, there will be less ego. In deep sleep, there are not many objects known, but one, the absence of everything. Therefore, ego in deep sleep is in the seed form. But, when it comes to the self,

Self is non objective.

How can there be a knower of the self,

The Self is self illumined. Colours and forms exist because of the eyes. In the kingdom of deaf people, sounds do not exist. To prove the existence of sound, ears are required. But, when it comes to ones own conscious existence, it being self illumined and established, there cannot be a knower of the self. Therefore, there being no object, no knower and only absolute conscious bliss remains. In the recognition of this, there is no 'I' born.

So the equation is, many things known over a long period of time, results in a very solid thick fat ego being born. Less things known for a short period of time, a weak ego is born. In deep sleep, there is one object called absence, so ego is in the seed form.

Absolute Self being non objective, zero objects known, therefore, no ego.

This subjective conscious existence requires to be known in this manner only. When objectivity is dropped fully, once and for all,

there is undivided, non dual conscious Self. In this there is no known- knowledge- knower trio.

In Self awareness, involvement of this is completely stopped.
This is different from Chitta Vritti Nirodhah.
There is no suspension of thoughts, but transcending thoughts.
Hence, no efforts involved.
When we focus attention in an objective manner,
the world along with mind is born.
When we are merely aware of breathing,
then it is called as the position of a witness.
'Sakshi Bhava'.
But here also there is a duality.

But, in this duality, being merely witness of breathing does not create any impressions of breathing on the mind as impressions are created on the mind when we interact with the world.

So, remain aware of breathing.
Don't concentrate on breathing.
When we remain aware of breathing,
slowly, slowly, awareness alone remains.
Inclusion of breathing in the awareness is also dropped.
Hence, when mere awareness of breathing is practiced,
the objectifying tendency in the knowledge is dropped.
Breathe deeper and deeper.
Recognize the process of body identification.
Discover how the awareness includes the tendency of objectification.
The body is included.
The world is born.

✦✦✦

MEDITATION 18

The first step is recognition of ourselves as someone other than the body.

This is an essential step to be taken.

Otherwise we will be stuck up in body identification.

What happens when we take this step?

Taking this step implies that the mind is no more under the stupor of 'tamoguna', or agitations because of 'rajoguna'.

Now, what is the reason that these two gunas influence the mind, which is basically 'satvaguna'. This happens because we give importance to material things.

The mind becomes matter oriented and then wrong is insisted upon as right. As a result, activities are initiated by 'rajoguna', and the mind becomes fully extrovert.

This happens because we have taken ourselves to be the body.

Thereafter, every thought, every action is for and concerning the body. To be saved from this calamity, the first step is accepting oneself to be other than the body.

Working on this principle, means accepting that the attributes of the body, do not belong to me.

The first attribute which defines the body is the shape and the form. So now we take the position of formless shapeless existence.

This is achieved by conscious relaxation of the body.

The mind soon gives up the shape of the body.

Keeping the body shape intact, when the seeker tries to pull or go within, all abnormal experiences begin. We don't want to do that.

Hence, imagine that you are outside the body and now relax the body. Remain outside. Relax the head, forehead, eyebrows, eyeballs, nose, cheeks, lips, chin. Relax relax relax. Relax the ears, neck from all around, hang down the shoulders, shoulder joints, upper arms, elbows, lower arms, wrist, palms and fingers.

Relax relax relax.

Let Meditation Happen

Now, go to the neck again, shoulders down from all the sides.

Like the water level in a container goes down when there is a hole in it, In the same manner, relax downwards from the trunk of the body. Go down slowly, all over, up to the waist. Relax the hips, thighs, calves, ankles, heels and toes.

As we have relaxed, to that extent, the mind has given up the shape of the body. As a result of this relaxation, the body is heavy on the base. This heaviness is because the mind has given up the hold on the body. Now, if you observe, the shape of the body, has become blurred, hazy to a great extent. Now, as much as the body has been disowned by the mind, to that extent, the 'tamoguna' is dropped.

Hence, the world of matter, now does not matter. The second problem is now of 'rajoguna'. Although the body has become still, the mind is still working. To quieten the 'rajoguna', remain aware of the breathing.

Don't pull yourself inside to create a pressure inside the cranium.

Body is already dropped. Stand apart. At this particular junction, one has to be extremely alert and aware.

Or else, we start becoming very concentrated and pull ourselves inside. Don't do that. If you feel that happening, remind yourself that you are outside the body.

Like the earth is in space, so also, the body is in me, the consciousness. Therefore, although something may tickle between the eyebrows, on the backside of the head, on the top of the crown, we have nothing to do with it. Simply remain aware of your being.

Now, our journey is from the changing to the changeless. Breathe deeper. Move your toes and fingers. Offer everything to the Lord.

✦ ✦ ✦

MEDITATION 19

If our mind is scattered here and there while we chant, then we have to become selective.

Only then is it easy to operate on the mind.

Operation of the mind means yoga abhyasa.

So, the mind must be available to us for operation.

If we are carried away by the force of thoughts, then we can't operate on the mind.

Like we do pranayama, yoga, upasana or chanting.

All these help us in bringing the mind together.

Purusha and prakruti, both of them are beginningless.

Like fire and burning power.

Prakruti has different phases to which it is caught.

Constant modification is constant about prakruti.

Prakruti, mahattattva, asmita, five sense organs, five organs of action, mind, pancha tanmatras, pancha maha bhutas, these 24 concepts constitute prakruti.

The mind is the one where, in even a thought the purusha gets reflected.

Thereafter, the thought, the reflection of purusha in the thought and the purusha himself, the three together become one entity.

If there is a thought of misery, the reflected consciousness in the thought getting identified, also becomes miserable.

The purusha, the reality, gives a feeling of reality to the miserable entity.

Thus, the thought on one side and the reality of purusha on the other side, together create an illusory reality called as an experience.

Hence, when the mind is sufficiently quietened, we are no more influenced by the tamoguna of prakruti or the dullness associated with it.

In that predominantly sattvik mind, the viveka khyati happens.

Purusha is consciousness, never changes.

Prakruti is constantly modifying.

When this knowledge takes place, thereafter, although the purusha is reflecting in the vritti, and the reflected purusha in the vritti experiences joys and sorrows, yet the purusha is independent of the vritti.

It neither gets identified with the thought, the misery or the miserable entity born in that thought.

The purusha tattva is really an illumination of the experiencer reflected consciousness in the thought and the infinite phenomenon.

This viveka khyati alone helps the seeker to be less and less effortful.

Efforts will become lesser, with the increase of viveka khyati.

The vigilance or the thought of the seeker, is not to get re-identified with the reflected consciousness in the thought.

Viveka khyati must ultimately become our second nature.

We no more express as the body. Rather we express through the body.

No more express as the mind, but only illuminating the modifications of the mind.

The purusha does not have any shape or form.

The reflected consciousness in the thought takes the shape and form of the thought.

With every thought, a new experiencer is born.

The pure consciousness is merely the illuminator of the content of the thought, the thought and the experiencer of the thought.

After this point, even the satvaguna is given up.

There are no thoughts. Hence, no experiencer of relativity.

This is chitta vritti nirodhah.

✦✦✦

MEDITATION 20

When we work on the mind, we are practicing 'yoga abhyasa'.

Working on the mind from the 'prakruti' or matter point of view, is a struggle.

But, when we work from the awareness point of view, there is no struggle.

From the 'prakruti' point of view, one first has to learn to be physically quiet.

Too much of bodily movements, strengthen body identification.

Therefore, just be quiet.

Don't move.

Nothing is more important than this auspicious moment.

Let us not miss it.

When we are steady, physically, the posture or the asana starts becoming stable.

As the mind starts giving up identification with the body,

the weight of the body on the base increases.

The body becomes fully relaxed.

The metabolic rate falls.

Breathing becomes slow and shallow.

We start by just remaining aware of our body and then aware of breathing.

This process leads to 'viveka khyati'.

Khyati means thought, understanding.

Viveka means discrimination.

So there is a clear distinct understanding between matter and awareness.

We take the position of awareness, then alone the asana, body, becomes like a wooden piece.

No movement.

If the shape of the body is not erased from the mind,

then we develop a kind of pressure inside our head, in the

Let Meditation Happen

eyeballs, or the body becomes tense.

Hence, when this happens, it is a warning, that we are getting identified with the body.

Like when there is pain in the body, it is a warning that something is wrong.

At such moments, walk out of your body, and take a view of your body from outside,

from all around.

Reconfirm to yourself that you are not inside the body, but the body is in you.

Hence, why suffocate in a small tiny body.

Like space remains undisturbed by the contents, so also, the mind must remain undisturbed by the contents, called as body etc..

The conscious space remains undisturbed by duality.

This solid conscious space is the ultimate reality.

✦✦✦

MEDITATION 21

In Patanjali Yoga Darshan, 'viveka khyati' is described which is 'samatwam yoga uchyate' in Gita.
Only 'chitta vritti nirodhah' is not important.
Every thought has got the content of name and form of an object, plus the existence of that object.
Existence is common for every object.
Name and form differ.
This existence which is common for all the objects, does not exclude us.
Because, we cannot experience our absence.
Hence, objectively our experience is recorded, recognized as name and form.
Subjectively, as the knower.
When names and forms which are known, when they are dropped,
means, when that criteria, which creates these differences,
that criteria of name and form, when it is dropped,
what remains is the existence.
When the names and forms which are known,
if they are dropped, there cannot be a knower,
because there is nothing to know.
Then, objectless awareness, is the truth.
Therefore, indifference to names and forms,
the total past, the imaginary future,
when this is practiced,
the mind starts disappearing.
In Yoga, we concentrate through the mind.
In Vedanta, we remain aware of our own presence.
Breathe deeper,
Move your toes and fingers,
Offer everything to the Lord.

✦✦✦

MEDITATION 22

Patanjali Maharshi tells us that 'chitta vritti nirodhah', is the goal of yoga.

It is through this chitta vritti alone, that we ride and go away from ourselves.

Riding on the chitta vritti, we cannot stay with ourselves.

How do we ride the chitta vritti?

It is by mere identification.

Just as a crystal kept near a red cloth, appears to be red, actually it is not.

In the same manner, we get identified with every thought, means that we appear to get identified.

In fact we are not.

Because, can the reflection in the mirror, be identified with the mirror?

The mirror being inert, the reflection is also an illusion, an appearance and inert.

In the same manner, in the inert thought, the purusha gets reflected and a fictitious non existing entity called as 'I' is born.

'I am happy', 'I am miserable' depending upon the kind of thought or vritti, 'I' is born.

Hence, when no thought, no vritti, no identification with the finite, then what happens to this purusha?

The same thing happens.

When the mirror is taken away what happens to our face?

Nothing.

In fact, when the mirror was in front of us, that time also nothing happened to us.

Therefore, to recognize this purusha, we have to quieten thoughts, and just recognize ourselves.

When there is identification with thoughts, we try to know, through the thoughts.

Let Meditation Happen

What is known through the thoughts is not reality.
It is only images.
But, these images help us in reaching the original.

In the same manner, when the thoughts are quietened, the purusha comes back home.

So, the first step in the practice of meditation, will therefore be, a full conviction that we have to suspend this thought formation.

When we are convinced, then we will work on that.
There are two practices to be done.
1] Abhyasa
2] Vairagya

Dispassion about the objectivity and recognition of the subject.

In fact, when we give importance to anything in this world, what happens is, thoughts are created about that thing.

Now, this is the thumb rule.
Giving importance to something, means thinking about that thing.
Importance is given in two ways.
Positive and negative.
Likes and dislikes.
Vairagya means remaining indifferent.

When our mind is spared and not dissipating its energy in the objective world, that energy is saved, conserved.

This energy is applied for being vigilant, alert, about the quality of the mind.

The study of scriptures, gives us directions, how to be our own self.

If you are not able to be indifferent to anything which is pulling you away, replace the theme.

eg: we engage the mind in being aware of our breathing.
So, the mind has some occupation.
This occupation does not take us away from ourselves.
Don't concentrate, observe or control the breathing.
Just be aware.
We should not concentrate on anything.
Concentration takes us away from ourselves to the object of

Let Meditation Happen

concentration.

About Self it is self awareness.

When we remain merely aware of breathing,

this knowing of breathing is neither through the senses, nor a feeling to the mind, nor as a concept through the intellect.

Being aware of breathing is 'vastu shunya'.

Breath is an object.

Breathing is not an object.

As we remain more and more aware, body is dropped from the mind.

Hence the weight of the body increases and settles on the base.

✦✦✦

MEDITATION 23

When we become aware of anything, that thing becomes shy and disappears.

When we become aware of somebody coming, about whom we were talking, immediately we drop that topic.

When we become aware that taking this food is harmful for our existence, we drop it.

But, when we are not aware, we are leading a life, just at the matter level.

Such people have no bad intention.

But, they become a source of nuisance to others,

because of not living in awareness.

Hence, this living in awareness is meditation.

So, when we sit for meditation, we become aware of our body.

The body becomes stand still.

When we become aware of our breathing, it slows thoughts.

What is that which brings this change?

This change happens because we no more identify with that.

When we become identified with anything, we start living mechanically.

This principle is applied even to the mind.

When we get identified with a particular thought, we get carried away by the thought.

In the words of Patanjali Maharshi, it is the viveka khyati, the clear cut appreciation, that purusha, the consciousness, cannot be attached to the prakruti, the matter or its modifications.

This purusha tattva is independent.

Prakruti by herself, cannot even change without the support of the changeless, the purusha, the consciousness.

In just being, there is no awareness of anything.

So, when you remain aware, all the movements of the prakruti stop.

Let Meditation Happen

Remaining indifferent is the first step.

Where the sense of otherness is yet valid.

We are indifferent about something other than the self, that is working from the platform of the mind.

When we remain aware, it is not indifference to the objective world, or thoughts,

but it is abidance in the subjective self, more intensely, we are aware of our just being.

We start withdrawing our identification with the body and the senses.

When identification with the body becomes minimum, the body becomes like a rock.

It will not move even a little bit.

This is called as conquering the asana.

Second thing is, dis identification from the senses.

The last faculty to disappear is ears.

Perceiving sounds is the strongest faculty.

The world enters our mind through the ears.

Hence, when the mind expresses through ears, hearing faculty is born.

Hence, we consciously withdraw our mind, away from the different sounds, as a first step.

Then we remain aware of silence.

Another technique of dis identification of the mind from the senses, is chanting of the Lords name.

Very slowly.

Inside the mind.

Om Namah Shivaya

Take a deep breath.

Observe the process of identification with the body and how again the sense of seperateness, sense of limited existence, sense of being a body, comes back.

✦✦✦

MEDITATION 24

There are two words.
Atma and anatma.
Atma is the one which we refer to ourselves.
Anatma is that which is referred to as other than the self.
This is the first stage, through which this discrimination goes.
Once we take this step, we start contemplating,
which is that, which we have taken to be ourselves?
What is that, which we take to be other than the self?
Now the discrimination begins.

For the most ignorant person, the possessions or worldly things, and various relations, they are considered to be oneself.

As a result, gain or loss in them, becomes the joy or sorrow.
But, is this a right understanding?
That which remains always, is called atma.
Do worldly things remain always?
No.
They cannot be atma.
Thus, we start with a cool mind.

To replace our identification with worldly things and people, we are told to practice 'samprajnat samadhi'.

So, instead of the people and possessions, outside, we fix the 'vigrah', idol of the Lord, or a picture, and to the exclusion of everything, only this is taken as a support.

When this becomes perfected, this one thought of the Lord cancels all the other objective thoughts.

Then we come to the second stage.
Now we no more practice it outside.
Now we practice it at the level of 'tanmatras'.

So, whatever we have read, heard about the glory of the Lord, that alone is the support for the mind.

These supports are reduced from many to minimum and from

minimum to one.

So first the stories, glories, devotees, then the Lords name and ultimately we come to one name of the Lord.

When this is practiced for sufficient period of time, then the seeker starts experiencing bliss, happiness in this chanting of the Lords name, to the exclusion of everything else. 'Ananda nugatah samprajnat samadhi'. Now, ultimately, the 'buddhi vritti' where the consciousness is reflected, is very clear, like a reflection in the mirror.

So, at this stage, one is able to clearly recognize the independent conscious existence. The reflection of this consciousness as 'chidabhasa' in the 'sattvik vritti', is clear. Now, the last step is, the purusha tattva, the conscious existence alone is independent.

This exposure to purusha tattva, strengthens the apara vairagya.

Now, the worldly objects, their thoughts, the joy in reveling them, everything is dropped.

Thought free consciousness is recognized.

By whom?

By the reflected consciousness in the 'sattvik vritti'.

This reflected consciousness in the 'sattvik vritti', alone comes in contact with the objective world, and behaves as a soul. But, when it is facing its own source, the vritti as if melts away, and the reflection disappears in its source. At this stage, because of the 'sattvik vritti', the knowledge of the outer sounds takes place but there is no disturbance felt, on account of that.

Because in the asmitanugata, the reflection and the vritti, they are one. The contents of the vritti are of no consequence. Hence, the mind is like a mirror.

Reflecting everything but not reacting.

When even this vritti, in which the sounds are heard, when even this quietens, the objective knowledge fully disappears. As it happens in deep sleep. But, there it is the 'tamoguni vritti' and here it is the 'satvaguni vritti'. Practice being completely indifferent to every perception and just be aware. Not aware of.

✦✦✦

MEDITATION 25

The periphery of our personality is the gross world and the gross body.

As long as this gross world and the gross body is the primary concern of our life,

we are far away from reality.

First we get involved with our gross body,

then with the help of the vehicles of thoughts, we go further from our own self.

This world and the body are constantly changing.

We are essentially unchanging reality.

When 'viveka khyati' takes place, means, when, by the apara vairagya,

sufficient dispassion about worldly enjoyments, mind remains predominantly sattvik.

In such a mind, the viveka khyati, the clarity of seperateness between the purusha and the prakruti, takes place.

When our understanding becomes distinctly subtle, it is no more under the influence of rajoguna and tamoguna, agitations or dullness.

But, now we are alert, vigilant and quiet.

Here the discrimination is possible.

The reflection of the sun, in a bucket of water, is exactly like the original sun.

It also throws light. In the light of the reflected sun, things are also illumined.

Therefore the original and reflected sun, they are almost the same.

However, if this reflected sun, tries to understand, see or know, the original sun, in his light, he will fail.

However when the reflected sun exposes itself, to the original sun, slowly water will evaporate, and the reflection of the sun will also disappear, and only the original sun will remain.

In the same manner, in the 'sattva vritti', in the thought which is predominantly sattvik, the reflection of consciousness creates an illusion of 'I'.

This 'I' has three components.

Original consciousness, the sattva vritti,

the thought which is predominantly sattvik.

And the reflection of the consciousness in this sattvik thought.

These three together are called purusha or the jiva.

It is one per head in every body.

However, like there is one original sun reflecting in millions of buckets of water, in the same manner, this jiva is not a reality.

This purusha who appears to be many, this is on account of many thoughts.

So, when in this Samadhi abhyasa, the seeker, that is these three factors together,

[Pure consciousness

Sattva vritti or sattvik thought,

reflection of consciousness in the sattvik thought]

becomes aware of the original consciousness, slowly even the sattvik thought disappears.

As long as the sattvik thought remains, it is 'samprajnat samadhi'.

When even the sattvik thought disappears it is 'asamprajnat samadhi'.

If sleepiness is overpowering, tamoguna is predominant.

If the perception of sounds, etc, disturb, or all unconcerned thoughts are erupting, then rajoguna is functional.

When satvaguna predominates, as in samprajnat samadhi,

the earlier two become subordinate and viveka khyati happens.

So, in this viveka khyati, the apara vairagya, dispassion about the gross world and subtle world enjoyments is the cause.

We have now come only in the satvaguna vritti.

The basic difference between the practice of meditation according to Vedanta and Yoga,

is, in the case of Vedanta, we straightaway hold on to the consciousness and come to discover that there is but one undivided homogeneous reality.

In case of yoga, we are quietening the prakruti.

After prakruti is quietened, then the purusha is separately recognized.

This separation of purusha and prakruti is kaivalya.

In Vedanta there is but one absolute reality and prakruti has no influence on this reality.

Like fire has no influence on the burning power.

The burning power does not influence fire.

'Brahma shraya maya'

it is not independent.

This prakruti, maya, avyakta, is independent in sankhya yoga, but it is dependent on purusha, the absolute reality.

✦✦✦

MEDITATION 26

'Drig' means the experiencer or the subject and 'drushya' is the object.

Therefore, the common understanding will be, as many persons, so many experiencers.

If there are 'n' number of persons, there are 'n' number of 'drigs', the subjects.

'Drushya' is one, because all of us are seeing the same thing, on the basis of this analysis.

The sankhya shastra says, 'prakruti is one and purushas are many'.

How many people stay in your house?

We start counting, mother, father, brother, sister, son etc.. Six of us are there.

In fact, father and husband are the same. Mother and wife are the same. Me and son are the same. Similarly, we are many, seer, hearer, smeller, thinker, etc..

But, if we re-evaluate our own experience, we come to know, that the happy, miserable, confused, decisive, successful, failure, we are so many personalities.

They are not real.

The child, teenager, youth, old.

They are not real.

The husband, wife, brother, sister.

They are not real.

There is one common substratum which appears to have become many, because of the many conditionings. So, 'drig brahma', the subject, is only one. Just as one person becomes many. Not really. One mind becomes many, not really. One conscious existence becomes many, not really. This one eternal, infinite subject alone, illuminates both the world that is present, as well as the absence of the world.

One absolute reality, the purusha, with the conditioning of total maya, is Ishwara.

Let Meditation Happen

One absolute reality, the same which expresses as Ishwara, expresses as the individual, the jiva, with reference to the panchakoshas.

When the jiva recognizes him to be the purusha, the purusha can be understood in two ways. One, the one expressing through the body, as a limited one and essentially who is infinite, is purusha.

So, when the gross and subtle body conditionings are transcended, the embodied one is discovered to be the infinite one. Space is one, because of many pots it becomes as if many.

But, it is not many. This space is our real nature. Space doesn't have shape, size, gender, date of birth. So, we take our position as space. Now, you can very clearly experience, that the body is dropped from the mind.

The pressure that we developed inside the body, also disappears. This vast, infinite space, which is formless, supports all the forms. The mental state supports all thoughts, not getting influenced by any one. Hence, there is no identification as a good thought or a bad thought, or their absence. See how effortlessly we have erased our shape and form, our thoughts.

Now, in this conscious state, unlike the mental and gross states, there are no contents. Waking, dream, deep sleep, Samadhi. They are within consciousness. Their coming and going does not leave any footprints on consciousness.

When we keep too many things in our bag, and try to accommodate everything, the bag develops pressure, on the sides.

But, all the contents kept in open space, develop no pressure of any kind. In the same manner, living as embodied, waker is the waking, dreamer is the dream, deep sleeper is the deep sleep, and samadhista is the Samadhi. These conditions are like trying to forcibly keep the contents inside, by applying pressure.

Hence, there is discomfort. Break the barrier of worry and thoughts. Like there is but one state of 'drig brahma'. There is but one infinite conscious existence.

✦✦✦

MEDITATION 27

When the goal is 'chitta vritti nirodhaha', our attention is on the world, thoughts and their modifications.

The rule is, whatever we give importance to, enters our mind.

That which we devalue, is deleted from the mind.

Hence, the seeker must be wise enough, to give only the required importance,

to the world, objects, relations and thoughts.

Patanjali Maharshi brings into his presentation, 'asamprajnat samadhi' which is possible also by 'ishwara pranidhan'.

So, this 'purusha visheshah ishwarah' helps the seeker, from getting away from matter and in entering the kingdom of consciousness.

Upto 'asamprajnat samadhi', we have only been talking about matter.

Thus, we remain only in matter.

When we remain in matter, the ego, asmita, ahankara, becomes stronger and stronger.

In fact, there is zero spiritual progress.

The individuality becomes very strong.

When our individuality becomes strong, we become as lone rangers in the world.

We cannot tolerate anything.

Hence, to get out of this, undue importance and value is given to matter and thoughts, which are also subtle matter.

We have to enter the halls of devotion.

Devotion to Ishwara.

Ishwara is by all these modifications of prakruti, 'aparamrustaha purusha vishesha'.

We have now changed our track.

From matter we have now come on another track of devotion.

A devotee of the Lord, seeks the Lord, consciousness.

When we start seeking consciousness, naturally, apara vairagya and para vairagya are bound to be.

When we seek the Lord through devotion, the struggle that a yogi goes for apara and para vairagya, this is not required.

eg: absence of enjoyment of this and other worldly things, a devotee only takes that which is offered to the Lord.

Not for his bhoga but as an offering.

So his indulgence becomes spiritual practice.

Whatever we do, it is for the Lord.

Not for the fulfillment of desires but as the will of God.

When this is practiced, 'viveka khyati' is also not required.

There is nothing to compare or discriminate between Ishwara and others.

Apara and para vairagya, both happen through Ishwara pranidhan, by offering ourselves to the Lord.

So, now chant a long OM and be so subjective that after Om is chanted, you merge in the Ishwara, the purusha vishesha, the consciousness.

The length of chanting and of silence that follows is almost equal.

Let us chant a few times.

Like in the presence of the bright sun, the light of a small candle disappears.

In the same manner, before the Lord, the small 'I' disappears.

This purusha vishesha is one infinite, untouched by prakruti and its modifications.

Like water is untouched by the ocean and waves.

'Asamprajnat samadhi' is a condition where there is no knowledge, no mind.

Because there is no mind there is no knowledge which contains I versus you.

This homogeneous undivided conscious self alone remains.

So, 'tadjapastad bhavanam' is to remain like space, which contains everything but is not disturbed by anything.

'Asamprajnat yoga', means, therefore, there is no objectivity left in the knowledge.

Let Meditation Happen

Because, now the prakruti has become unmanifest in the purusha.

Therefore, this experience is objectless, means objectivityless awareness.

We are not aware of.

We are awareness.

Breathe deeper.

Observe how body identification takes place.

Unless we transcend body identification, the thoughts about the world, will never stop.

What happens in 'asamprajnat samadhi' is only this.

Purusha separates from the prakruti.

Thoughts and identification with the body is given up.

✦ ✦ ✦

MEDITATION 28

One day a seeker asked me, 'What is the meaning of atma chintan?'
Is it contemplation or thinking about the self?
We cannot think about the self, so, what is atma chintan?
I told him, 'Anatma chintan abhava'.
Meaning, when we totally stop thinking about that which is anatma, which is not the self.
So, we first have to find out that which is not the self.
All that is known is not the self.
In this list of known, we start from space, air, fire, water and earth.
Their various combinations. This world of duality.
Up to here it is fine.
We don't think.
Because, we never think about space.
We never think about air or fire.
So, let us not think about objects.
We must not allow their entry in the mind.
Objects enter our mind, first like an object enters the mirror as a reflection.
Up to this stage, the object will not make our mind as their home.
After the object has entered our mind as reflection, then the second stage of the mind begins.
The mind interacts with that perception.
In terms of giving positive or negative value to that object.
Positive value is liking, leading to attachment.
Negative value is disliking, leading to hatred.
These impressions of likes and dislikes are seeds for our thinking about the world.
So, when the mind is busy thinking outwardly, it cannot think about the self.
Hence, we have to consciously live in this world, where perceptions are not followed by projections, leading to likes and dislikes.

Let Meditation Happen

This is called vairagya.
Second will be abhyasa.
Now, the mind is free from objective involvement.
We start chanting AUM.
A long AUM with an equally long silence.
Those who are unable to do this, chant Hari Aum.
Try to increase the gap between two chantings.
Now whether you are chanting or whether stray thoughts are coming in your mind, take the position of mental space.
Mental space is that which supports thoughts, but doesn't get influenced by thoughts.
Because, mental space is indifferent to all thoughts.
You must have observed that now the body has become more relaxed. As if the tension of the body has gone.
The weight on the pin bones has increased.
There is a kind of release from body identification.
Because, in the position of mental space, thoughts become impotent.
Hence, the body is dropped from the mind.
Now your experience is like being as vast space.
Now your mind is merged in the infinite and thoughts disappear.
Like when you move a hot iron on the cloth, the wrinkles on the cloth disappear.
Remain vigilant that the mind doesn't slip back into objectivity.
So, take a position that you are non specific existence.
Not somebody.
Not anybody.
But, nobody.
When we remain vigilant and alert, the mind may entertain anything, but we catch the mind, like an invigilator catches the copying student.
When we are unable to totally suspend thoughts, because of lack of apara vairagya,
the only help is Ishwara pranidhan.

MEDITATION 29

The working of the mind, the creation of an experiencer with every experience and the birth of an illusion of ego, with the passage of time, these are worth knowing and then controlling.

What happens with every experience is, every perception is accompanied with our interaction with the perception.

Our interaction to the perception is the cloth, a dress, a uniform, put on the body of perception.

If our interaction or projection on a particular object, is that it is good, it is required, it is valuable, it will help me in getting completeness, it is a source of happiness, without this object life is incomplete, what is the use of living without this object, this is the cloth, ornament, make-up we superimpose on the original thought of perception.

This could be either positive or negative.

Such a well-dressed, properly made up thought, dances in our mind.

Because it is our own creation,

we give value and importance to such a well dressed thought.

This happens in case of every thought.

Like God created man, and the tailor gives us a dress to make us a gentleman.

In the same manner, the thought of perception is in prakruti, and the different dresses and ornaments are not created by God or prakruti, these are our creations.

Thus, with every additional thought, to which we have given value, importance and existence, we start becoming weaker and weaker.

Thoughts start becoming stronger and stronger.

It is like, we have children and as time passes, instead of us controlling or governing them, in old age, it is the other way around.

The children dictate and control us.

The same thing happens in our mind.

Let Meditation Happen

When you sit quietly, you can very distinctly experience these two factors.

1] The objective aspect of thought, perception and dress on thought.
2] The owner of thought.

Because we give importance to them, they become strong and we become weak.

Now, if you are clear up to here, what is the meaning of witness?

When any thought erupts, and comes with the make-up, our approach should be, we have to be indifferent.

Remaining indifferent means giving zero value to the presence or absence of any thought.

So, when we give zero value, the thought starts dying.

Because they were gathering strength, borrowing existence from us.

When we are indifferent, thoughts start becoming weak.

Starvation of existence to objective thoughts, if it is continued, slowly, the object disappears from our knowledge.

When the object disappears, the thought along with make up, also disappears.

Now, this is the state of the objective thought.

What happens to the subjective thought that was remaining indifferent?

In the absence of the objective thought, the subjective thought also starts starving.

This starvation leads to pruning and removing the fatty layer of thought on this absolute I.

So, when we remain indifferent, the objective thoughts become minimum source of disturbance, and the thought aspect of the I thought starts receding.

Ultimately, the thoughts disappear, and with the disappearance of thoughts, only thought free conscious existence remains.

As we start remaining indifferent, to every thought that erupts, the frequency of thoughts falls.

The intensity of thoughts also weakens.

Let Meditation Happen

The asana becomes firm and steady.

Breathing is slow and shallow.

The weight of the body on the base increases.

Now, we remain indifferent to every objective thought.

When all the thoughts disappear, absence becomes the object.

Absence of thoughts.

When absence becomes the object, we enter sleep.

That is the reason many seekers fall asleep while meditating.

Their falling asleep is because of absence of thoughts.

Hence, when objectivity of thought is rejected, don't end up in absence.

Thought disappearing with only one thought remaining, of absence.

This thought free I again gets identified with this absence, and disappears in deep sleep.

Hence now we work on the subject.

So, the Self is 'sat', ever present.

'Chit', thought free knowledge.

'Sat' and 'chit' being one, there is absolute absence of otherness, the objectless awareness called 'ananda', or bliss.

Now our experience is like space.

No form, no beginning, no end.

Although everything is no, no, no, yet there is no absence.

That which remains after negating everything, even the negator is negated, the last trace of thought vanishes.

Just for a few seconds you remain non-alert, and you are taken for a ride, by thoughts.

We cannot afford even one moment of being not alert.

✦ ✦ ✦

MEDITATION 30

We will practice fixing our mind for a longer period of time on one tattva. There are 24 tattvas according to sankhya. Prakruti, mahattattva, asmita, 11 indriyas, pancha tanmatras and pancha mahabhutas. We can take one tattva from each group.

For eg: take one object, like the limited expression of tanmatra, gandha, smell. When I am smelling a flower, there is no other smell at that moment. Because our attention is only on the finite expression of gandha tattva. So, Patanjali Maharshi tells us, that 'No, not the smell of an object. But, the gandha tattva itself'.

So, how do we go from the finite or limited expression of gandha tattva in an object to the nescient, unqualified principle of gandha, the smell. If we do this, the mind will move away from the effects or the expressions, to the cause or that which was expressing.

So, the gandha, the smell, is a flower, an object. Gandha tattva is far beyond that. Therefore, the mind which was expressing as the receiver of the smell, through the nose, was getting caught up in the flower. But, now the mind is withdrawn from the flower, and remaining only at the 'jyanendriya', the instrument which is able to receive every smell.

Thus, we take one step towards withdrawal from the objective world. Because, now the mind has discovered that it is the source of all experiences of smell and not the object outside.

This happens with any one object, and we have first hand experience. As a result, the mind stops running from one object to another object. Now, try this with one object. On the tip of the nose, if you focus your attention, you will catch the gandha samvit.

At the tip of the tongue, rasa samvit. At the root of the mouth cavity, taluni roop samvit. In the centre of the tongue, sparsh samvit. At the base of the tongue, shabda samvit. Try it out with whichever tattva you are naturally inclined towards.

✦✦✦

MEDITATION 31

When we perceive anything......
When we know an object........
That object has five different qualities.
Although the object is one.........
We see that object because of the five qualities with five senses in five different ways.
When one object is seen in five ways............
Samsara is created.
Hence, we were told, to hold on to any one tattva.
When we see colour and form of a flower, not any other quality of the flower, we have already narrowed down from five to one.
Now the next step.
When we recognize the colour and form of the flower, it is recognized as colour and form of something.
Not the principle of colour and form, that is rupa tan matra.
So, we have to drop even the colour and form of the flower, and do the dharana on the palette inside our mouth cavity.
On the floor of the mouth, is the tongue, like a carpet, and above in the roof is the place of rupa tanmatra.
At the base of the tongue is the shabda tanmatra.
Now, do the dharana wherever you want.
At the tip of the nose, gandha tanmatra.
At tip of tongue, rasa tanmatra.
On the talu, rupa tanmatra.
At the centre of tongue, sparsh tanmatra.
Now we bring our attention without any tension, to one of these points.
Try to nail the mind to that point.
First the mind will run here or there.
But slowly it will happen.
Selecting one or the other point, for the separation of the mind,

Let Meditation Happen

we will have to individually discover, which is natural for us.

Whether it is the pancha maha bhutas, the heart, the asmita or the formless conscious existence.

When you do it, you will discover, in case of fixing the mind on one of these points of prakruti, we remain indifferent to consciousness.

Once our mind is sufficiently controlled, then we can barely recognize this conscious existence as independent of matter.

The matter along with its modifications disappears.

Recognize the difference between concentration and awareness. Viveka khyati then becomes easier.

✦ ✦ ✦

MEDITATION 32

We have seen in our vedantic text, 'Sadachar', the meaning of the 'Gayatri mantra, upasana, anushthana'.

Chanting is done at different levels according to the seeker.
Initially, we start only by chanting the mantra correctly,
and may not be hundred, thousand times,
But, may be only a few times.
Say, eleven times.
And when we become very clear about every syllabyl that we chant or utter,
and if it is done with complete surrender to the divine principle,
That is indicated through the 'Gayatri mantra',
then even if we do not know the meaning,
the impact will be seen on our mind.
The mind will start remaining quieter and steady.
And after this is done,
the mantra chanting is suspended.
Then this mantra gives us some data for contemplation.
Please remember, we are not interested in putting a brake to thinking,
but, you want to go beyond the thinking
and not thinking.
For that,
Let us chant the 'Gayatri mantra' a few times.
As you have been told,
'Gayatri mantra' is chanted like this,
'Om bhur bhuva swaha'
Om- Om is the divine syllabyl, port,
which gives sanctity and meaning to the mantra.
Bhur bhuva swaha- these are called 'vyanatis'.
These 'vyanatis' are required to be added if we are chanting the mantra.

Let Meditation Happen

If these are absent, then the chanting is said to be incomplete.
So please chant slowly.
'Om bhur bhuva swaha,
tat savitur varenyam,
bhargo devasya dhimahi,
dhiyo yo nah prachodayat.'
Chant eleven to fifteen times.
Now we will chant again.
But, this time, instead of the mind hanging without a support and after a few chants, the mind running into different thought patterns,
we shall fix the mind in one place,
and that place is the center of our chest,
where the ribs join the middle cartilage.
It is here that the consciousness expresses as mind.
From here the 'I' is born.
The mind starts coming out from this point, remains, and goes back there alone.
Thus, the mind does not have to run around the world.
When we start, we will feel that the sound begins from this point.
Chant a few times and you will see that the mind has quietened to a great extent.
Hence, even the minute sounds of the insects,
which were normally not recognized,
even they have become perceptive.
And as we continue, more and more silence,
the sounds will no more disturb us.
So, taking the support of the sounds,
what we were doing was ' veekshan '
All other objects were discarded,
only 'shabda' and in that also, only one mantra.
Now, here there were three things,
'shabda, artha and jnana',
Like, when you say 'cow',

cow is the word, [shabda]
animal, [artha]
and the knowledge about cow,[jnana].
Similarly, the mantra, the shabda,
the meaning of this mantra.

If enquired into the meaning and knowledge of this mantra, the Lord is practised as upasana and that is the root self.

The meaning is, the Lord Sun in the sky or the self is all pervasive.
When the mind becomes one with this understanding,
the mind has become the sun.
The shabda and the knowledge, both are dropped,
and the meaning of the mantra, Lord Sun, alone remains.
Initially, when we chant,

at that time, the words, the thought and the meaning of the words, all are mixed up.

However, this is the first step.
Then you have excluded all other things.
As we approach the meaning of the mantra,
the words and the thought of the words,

the knowledge disappears and the mind is fully identified with the object.

Here, Lord Sun.
With this understanding the 'Gayatri mantra' should be chanted.

✦ ✦ ✦

MEDITATION 33

Mind is born with every thought, as long as the mind is, thoughts are.

Our experience of relative existence will not disappear and in the relative existence there is zero possibility of absolute bliss, unless we look upon the relative existence just as an illusion.

Like the mirage water does not disturb us,

On the contrary, we enjoy the sight.

But, when this is not known, the doer runs after the mirage water and collapses to death.

In the same manner, we should look upon this same world as a mere projection of the mind.

Therefore, 'sadhana', meditation, is that you are consciously after the annihilation of the mind.

But, who wants one's own annihilation?

Therefore, the mind keeps on giving us beautiful suggestions.

Either in terms of past experiences or in terms of future imagination.

The moment the mind comes in the present, it is no more. This trick of the mind has to be understood.

Therefore, like we are sitting, let us not invoke the participation of the mind in meditation.

Right in the beginning, just be aware of the body or the 'prana'.

What is the difference between knowing the body and being aware of the body?

When we know the body, the body becomes a reality and our identification with the body becomes firm.

When we are aware of the body, slowly, slowly, awareness increases because we are not with the body, we are with our own awareness.

So, in these two aspects, knowing the body, we are with the body.

Being aware of the body, we are with the awareness.

When we remain aware, like most of you are now, without

any special efforts, your posture has become firm at the base and vertically the body has become steady.

You have not done anything to the body.

Not even adjusted your posture.

Being aware of anything means, mere illuminating that thing without getting identified with it.

Like, light is aware of our presence here, But, our presence or absence does not influence the light.

In the same manner, Remaining aware of the body, we slowly live the two, Dis-identification with the body and remaining in just awareness.

We thus bypass the mind.

So, the second aspect is the habitual thinking in the mind.

Now, the same technique applies.

Let us not be the witness of the thoughts, but, let us be just aware, like the sounds of the vehicles on the road.

They come and go.

We remain undisturbed.

Now see, your habitual unwanted thinking has fallen tremendously.

Recognize this awareness, as we recognize space.

Objects keep moving in space.

But, space does not move.

Similarly, perceptions, experiences, keep going through consciousness without touching it.

You will observe one specific aspect of the mind.

We may not be disturbed by sounds or any external perception, but, we get carried away in the floods of thoughts.

So, just remain aware of the gross and subtle.

No participation. No interaction.

✦ ✦ ✦

MEDITATION 34

'Tapas swadhyay ishwara pranidhan kriya yogah'
'Tapas swadhyay ishwara and pranidhan' all of them together constitute 'kriya yoga'.

It is meant for those who are still carrying the load of 'samsara'.

They have got lots of complaints about everything.

So, what can be done with these complaining persons?

They have to be kept busy.

Therefore, it is said, that start doing something.

This is what our scriptures say.

Like, in old age, people have nothing to do, so, they complain or worry.

Therefore, they are told, start doing 'japa', start writing 'shri ram jay ram jay jay ram' with all devotion.

And when we start doing it on a regular basis, what happens inside our system is our mind, which was going here and there by default, that stops and then by constant impressions of 'japa', on the mind, the earlier habits are broken.

Unless we break our earlier habits, we will not be able to proceed further.

Therefore 'Tapas swadhyay ishwara and pranidhan', is meant for breaking our present lifestyle and changing into the God oriented lifestyle.

Therefore, we are told to do tapasya.

According to yogis, tapasya is 'pranayamah paramam tapaha', There is no better 'tapas' than pranayama.

So, we will do pranayama.

Then devotees are told, 'tajjapah tadartha bhavanam', Keep on chanting Aum and after you chant for sometime, then, 'tadartha bhavanam', Then do the bhavana, thinking on the meaning of Aum.

So, first the seeker chants Aum,
and then he does the bhavana.

Let Meditation Happen

Today, we will chant Aum few times, then we will do 'tadartha bhavana', what is the meaning of Aum.

Then we will get to a point, where we can practice 'viveka khyati'. Separating 'purusha' from 'prakruti'.

We will do these stages, step by step.

Now, when the mind is a bit settled down, engage this mind in 'tadartha bhavanam' AUM has three letters.

'a', 'u', 'm' followed by silence.

Silence is not created.

Sound is created.

In silence, sound may be absent, but we are present.

There is no absence of our being. This is the data.

So, 'tadartha bhavana', one kind of contemplation is this, when we chant Aum, in that Aum, there is sound on the surface, below which there is silence and this is illumined by the presence.

Now, in this chanting, where we chant Aum, we leave the silence and enter the sound.

When Aum is over, again silence takes over.

Thus, only the Aum sound has a beginning, stay and end.

But, silence is ever the same.

Now, this is one data.

Second one is, silence and sound, they are mutually exclusive.

If there is sound, silence is not, if there is silence, sound is not.

But, there is one common denominator, which illuminates both the sound and silence.

This common denominator unlike the sound and silence, not opposed to both of them, this unopposed conscious existence, unopposed sound and silence together, this is the meaning of Aum.

In this, sounds are not disturbances and silence is not pleasurable.

Nothing is added by sounds.

Nothing is lost in silence.

'Tadartha bhavana', this is 'artha', The reality indicated by Aum.

✦✦✦

MEDITATION 35

Life is a steady, slow and a directional process.
Either we go away from us or we come back to us.
Both these directions require knowledge.
First step is knowledge.
Second step is understanding.
Third step is conviction.
Fourth step is converting conviction into experience.
Then the individual as itself disappears and the absolute starts expressing through us.
Therefore, either we go by this path, or we follow the beaten path, which is followed by our forefathers.
Culture, tradition etc..
The idea is evolution not revolution.
There are no jerks.
There are no sudden turns.
Once we have started on this path,
our first destination is attainment of body dis-identification.
Keeping this as a central goal,
we continue to lead our life as before.
No change.
And when we work on this body dis-identification,
then we start our subtle journey,
which will change us from within but outside we will be the same.
When we are living as body in the relative world,
we must follow the rules and regulations as given in our scriptures.
When we take ourselves to be the soul,
then we are a part of the lord.
And when we take ourselves to be a substratum of the relativity,
then everything ends.
Therefore, mere intellectualization is not advisable.
So, we work on this.

We are someone other than the body means what?
And what will that experience be like?
What will be the experience of bodyless existence?
What will be the consequence,
when we come to realize ourselves to be other than the body?
Working on this is meditation.
Anybody cannot do this.
One has to be qualified.
That qualification is 'Tapas swadhyaya ishwara pranidhanam'.
Understanding through purified mind and an untrained mind give contrary results.

Thinking and contemplation is not argument and logic.
When we start,
first, body stability,
then breathing,
quality must be slow and shallow,
then the bhavana, being other than the body, means what?
So, you can try one principle.
Other than the body means being formless.
So, all the shapes and the forms must disappear from the mind.

✦ ✦ ✦

MEDITATION 36

'Avidya, asmita, raga, dwesha, abhinivesha',
These five are notions born out of our not being aware of our own being.
Because of this lack of living in awareness, we start leading a life of mechanical existence.
Whenever we do anything mechanical,
the charm is lost.
The boredom begins.
Life becomes a burden and tiring.
 On the contrary,
when we live more and more in awareness, the world loses its potency to disturb us.
We are able to observe the various moods of the mind
and according to that mood of the mind, we practice meditation.
Sometimes, if the mind is too dull,
then a little more of pranayam.
If the mind is a little more agitated,
then chanting some 'stotra', a chapter of 'Gita', or chanting a mantra,
and thus, we start living more and more in the present.
One of the most important aspect is not to reduce the practice of meditation to a physical dream.
Second thing is,
what was practiced earlier,
the same thing is repeated,
and thus we live more in memory and thoughts,
rather than living in awareness.
Therefore, do not make a memory of the meditation.

✦✦✦

MEDITATION 37

When we have a clear goal as to the destination we have to reach, both within the limits of time and our means, then there are no difficulties.

Then there are no questions.

If our reaching the goal is the top priority.

And if we have no goal, no destination to reach, no time frame, no road map, then like a jogger, we jog through life.

And again come back to the same house of body identification.

Hence, we cannot afford to forget the first destination in meditation and spiritual life is body dis-identification.

Because the whole waking world begins with the body identification.

If we are convinced of this goal, then we will find out the means. If we are not convinced of this goal, then we will find out excuses.

Like when we are convinced, we have to reach a particular destination, then we will find out how we have to reach there, not the other way, how we cannot reach !

So, as of now, what is our asset in life?

Our own notions.

Our notion about ourself.

The world, God and spiritual practice.

Now, we have lived sincerely as body.

Now, let us pause for a moment, and evaluate our identity as body. We will come to know that the body has never been ours,

nor was it created by us.

So, the first step will be: even if we don't have the experience, let us pretend as if we are walking out of the body.

Look at your body just as you look at someone else's body.

Now, keep this position that you are outside the body.

Now, work on this position. What exactly does that mean?

If our existence is independent of the body,

then the attribute of body does not belong to us.

Therefore, now our position is formless, beginning less, endless and modification less awareness.

Now, if you have taken this position correctly, the body will disappear from your knowledge.

The concept of inside or outside will also disappear.

When the mind runs in different directions, you will observe that they are either memories, future planning or worries.

At this stage, the mind is struggling for it's survival.

When the mind was identified with the body, it had some support, to think in relation to the body and that support is given up.

Now, it is digging the past or predicting the future.

Hence, we have to come to the present.

There is one thing in our life, that we do only in the present.

That is our breathing.

Hence, we remain aware of breathing.

If the mind is running too much in the past and future, then when it comes in the present, simply be aware.

Remaining just aware of breathing is called as 'vriksha pranayama'.

When our breathing becomes slow and shallow, the mind is becoming weak.

And it merges in consciousness.

When we remain aware of breathing, we don't force or do anything to the breathing. When we concentrate on breathing, 'asmita' is born.

The doership is the bondage. Hence, let no attempt to do something be encouraged.

When one remains just aware, 'Prakruti', here the mind, will take it's own sweet time. Remaining aware means being indifferent.

This living in awareness is not limited to meditation, but, it is carried on in life. Meditation is left behind. This eternal awareness, knowing is being.

✦ ✦ ✦

MEDITATION 38

Patanjali Maharshi says that the Yoga Shastra goes through four stages.

First, diagnosis of the disease.

Second, cause of the disease.

Third, medicine for that disease.

Fourth, liberation from the disease.

So, what is the disease?

The disease is 'aham', 'samsara' or relative existence.

Cause of the disease is identification of the 'purusha' with the 'prakruti', thereby creating a fictitious entity called as the soul, the 'jiva'. Therefore, when dis-identification of the 'purusha' with the 'prakruti' takes place, then only the seed of 'samsara' is removed and moksha takes place.

So, what is spiritual practice?

That by which 'purusha' and 'prakruti' remain separated.

This illusion of the 'jiva' can only be removed by understanding.

Like the illusion of the mirage, illusion of sunrise and sunset, illusion of a blue, dome shaped sky, is removed.

It becomes non-consequential, because it is recognized as an illusion. Recognition of an illusion as an illusion, is the only way to transcend the illusion.

Hence, let us see how this illusory 'I' is created. In every thought, Knowledge of the object of the thought, the thought of the object and the knower of the thought and object, these three things are created.

The object cannot exist without the other two and so on. So, when we say, 'Hari Aum', Here, knower number one was born. Then there is a gap. Then we say it again. Knower number two is born.

The first knower in the first thought has no relation whatsoever with the second knower.

Then what is the illusion?

Let Meditation Happen

The illusion is, that the knower is one and the thoughts are many. But, what is happening is, many independent knowers borrow their existence from the common continuous existence.

So the continuity of the conscious existence,

like the thread, and many individual knowers like individual flowers, are brought together and a fictitious entity called as the ego or a garland is created.

Without the thread, garland cannot exist.

In the same manner, this continuous conscious existence is the reality and individual knowers have a temporary existence.

What do we see between the two flowers?

We can see two things.

Either absence of the flower or the presence of the thread.

In the same manner, when one experience is over, all the three components of the experience disappear.

When the second experience is yet to begin, in between there is objectless awareness.

Like, in a garland, there is flowerless thread.

Further, one isolated single flower cannot make a garland.

Hence, when we stay in the present, without the past or the future, we can talk in or at only the finite. In infinite, neither is there a thought or action.

Being infinite cannot be comprehended, hence cannot be spoken of, cannot be thought of. To remain in this present, remain aware of breathing. Slowly breathing will become very non-distinct. That time we are nearing the thread of the conscious existence. Don't concentrate on the breathing. Simply 'remain'.

✦✦✦

MEDITATION 39

When we become somebody, it is at that point that thoughts begin erupting.

So, that point of somebody on the surface of the mind is like a mouth of a volcano of thoughts.

Now, we have to understand this very clearly and experience it.
Let us do one experiment.
Take the position that you are an officer, husband, wife, sister.
After you take that position,
you will see that, slowly slowly,
thoughts will start coming out.
Flowing as that Mr. Somebody.
Now, do this and then I will tell you the next step.
Now, stop.
Now, do this second thing.
Imagine that you have to go to a fair.
To see the fair.
Now stop.
Now, see these two things.
When you became somebody,
when you are due to go to a fair,
See the related thoughts.
Now, third experiment.
If you are a man or a woman,
only that much identification.
I am a man or I am a woman.
With this identification, leave the mind there.
Now change the position.
If you are a man, think you are a woman.
If you are a woman, think you are a man.
Now, all these experiments very clearly demonstrate,
that our thoughts are always in relation to something.

Let Meditation Happen

Therefore in relative existence,
thoughts are bound to be.
Now, this same principle is further extended,
as a foundation of our experiences.
When we are identified with the body,
the waking experience begins.
When we identify with the modification of the mind, dream experience begins.
When identification is with the absence of these two, waking and dream,
then deep sleep begins.
If these experiences are mutually exclusive, waker has no entry in dream and so on.
But, there is a common denominator which illuminates all the three experiences.
And remains untouched by any one of them.
This conscious existence, like space, is not the creation of the mind.
Because the creation of the mind is destroyed.
Our position is like space.
Infinite, formless, modificationless, supports all the contents but not influenced by any one of them.
Like, mental space supports all the thoughts,
but, is not influenced by any one of them.
This conscious space is solid space.
Every time you get carried away by thoughts,
catch yourself at that time,
trace back the path by which you were drifted.
You will invariably end up in the fact, that you had become somebody.
This principle must go deep into our understanding.
As somebody, you cannot have freedom from thoughts.
As nobody, you cannot have thoughts.
Somebody is a specific finite temporary condition.

Let Meditation Happen

Nobody is infinite absolute existence.
Space is like nobody.
Our room space is like somebody.
Interior thought is like somebody.
Waker, dreamer is somebody.
Your conscious existence is like nobody.
Tat twam asi.
That thou art Come to recognize that.
Eyes are not opposed to any form or color.
Ears are not opposed to any sound.
Mind is not opposed to any thought.
Because, they are not influenced by their respective fields.
So is the case with conscious existence.
In the waking and dream, nothing is added.
In the deep sleep and samadhi, nothing is removed.
This unopposed ever present conscious existence is the reality.
Therefore, no struggle, effortless, uninfluenced,
conscious existence is hidden as if behind waking, dream, deep sleep and samadhi.
Hence, no reaction or opposition to anything in this world.
The rule is, illuminator is not influenced.
The doer is always influenced.
If our meditation is an act of meditation,
then we will be lost.
If meditation is not an act but through discrimination,
being aware of this phenomena,
sounds come and go,
ears are the same.
Waking, dream come and go, consciousness is the same.
Take a breath or so.
Slowly increase the depth.
Move your toes and fingers.
Offer everything to the Lord.
Don't make a memory of the experience.

MEDITATION 40

When life is understood from the individual unit point of view,
the understanding, perceptions, experiences, all remain influenced by the unit of individuality.
With reference to whom life is looked at.
Example: if we look at life from the point of view of a child, a teenager, a middle aged and an old person,
these four individualities will have different understandings of life.
All of them are right as well as wrong.
Right, because they are talking of their immediate experiences.
Wrong, because they are caught up in a particular angle of looking at life.
Hence, meditation is, living in that awareness where,
our individual experiences are reviewed from the totality of the experiences of life.
When we do this,
what happens is,
our individual joys and sorrows,
they no more influence us,
as this is the same thing that is happening,
in the whole expression of life.
When we develop this faculty,
looking at our individual experiences, from the totality of life expressions,
we are practicing witnesshood.
So, we illuminate the experience,
but, refuse to get influenced by that experience.
Till we don't get influenced by any experience,
we don't create an impression on the mind.
The mind is not strengthened.
The mind is not fattened.
Living in awareness is living in the utter present.

Let Meditation Happen

The only thing that happens in the present,
is our own breathing.
We don't breathe with respect to past or future.
Hence, remain aware of the breathing.
Don't concentrate.
Simply, know that breathing is happening in you.
The body is in the space.
So, also the body allows the breathing,
and the space is in this absolute self.
Breathe a little deeper.
Two three times, slowly,
Move your toes and fingers.
Offer everything to the Lord.

✦ ✦ ✦

MEDITATION 41

As long as there is an urge to do something, we will even do meditation.

That urgency to do something is holding us with the body identification, very firmly.

We have a notion that by doing something like meditation, worship, charity, yoga, by doing something we are going to create a reality. In fact, after knowing, nothing remains to be known or done. Because knowing is being. Like, when a thing is left from the hand, it falls on the ground. In this Newton has not created the Law of Gravity. In the same manner, we just have to know, that one mind becomes many.

Because of the five organs of perception and five organs of action, but, the mind is one. Behind the plurality of expression, there is one mind. Similarly, behind the plurality of life, expressing through different bodies, there is but one conscious existence.

Then what will be our spiritual practice or meditation?

It will be merely living in awareness.

Like when one mind expresses through different senses or organs, there is no mutual competition and their fields are well demarcated.

There is no overlapping of their duties.

In the same manner, when one consciousness is expressing through different bodies, there is no competition and their fields of activity are well demarcated.

If we cannot just Be because of the earlier force of habit momentum, then be aware of breathing. Without altering it. We must not miss a single breathing. The mind will go in some channel of thinking. Again, by understanding and by educating the mind, come back to being aware of breathing.

✦ ✦ ✦

MEDITATION 42

Consciousness cannot be influenced by matter.

In pure consciousness, of only matter, there is no 'samsara'.

The matter, namely thoughts, become enlivened by the reflection of consciousness in the thoughts.

Now, let us understand reflection, clearly.

Reflection is understood as the reflection of the sun in a bucket of water. Or as a reflection in the mirror.

There is another way that we use this word.

A cultured childhood is reflected in present behaviour.

How a person is in the present, is an indication of how he was as a child.

There also we use the word reflection.

Similarly, good training and practice, is reflected in his performance. Electricity is reflected in the bulb as light.

So, reflection means expression.

So, in the absolute 'purusha', Consciousness, there is no 'samsara', so in the matter.

But, this consciousness reflects, meaning expresses through the body, as 'spandana', or a throb.

Because of this throb of consciousness, waves of thoughts are created, in the consciousness.

So, consciousness with thoughts becomes 'chitta', and when this 'chitta' includes any particular object in it's womb, then it is called thought. In this thought, there are two aspects.

Objective aspect of thought which removes the ignorance about the object.

And knowledge is created. Subjective aspect of thought where owner of knowledge is born. 'I know this is an object.'

Thus, for each experience in each thought, the objects are separate from other thoughts and knowledge.

Separate from other thoughts and knower, and are also separate

Let Meditation Happen

from thoughts to thought.

It is here that we get confounded.

We take the many knowers and the underlying continuous consciousness and together create an illusion of 'jiva', the soul.

Hence, the advice given is, remain in the present.

So, there is only one knower with one thought.

Example: chant Hari Aum.

When we repeat the same thought,

Although they are many,

but, the content of all the thoughts is the same.

Then we will be able to appreciate, that this one conscious existence supports many knowers, born in many thoughts.

But, this conscious existence is common.

One, without a second.

This clear discrimination between conscious existence, 'purusha', and the reflection of 'purusha', in thought, producing an illusory knower, the discrimination between these is termed as 'viveka khyati', by Patanjali Maharshi.

Hence, when we remain merely the illuminator of thoughts without getting influenced by the content of the thoughts, we are in a position with conscious existence.

This is 'samprajnat samadhi asmitanugata'.

As we practice this 'viveka khyati', for a longer time, the old habit of getting identified with every thought and every thing, starts decaying.

And we no more have the wrong notion of our identity. As conditioned consciousness. In 'viveka khyati', the mind is still living. Being predominantly 'sattvik'.

Therefore, pure and undisturbed, the 'sat' existence and 'sattva', they are the same. 'Sat', the absolute reality and 'sattva' the pure knowledge. Like we learn how to balance a cycle, in the same manner we learn to balance these two.

✦✦✦

MEDITATION 43

The order in which we fill our suitcase,
we cannot empty it in the same order.
If we want to empty it, it will be in the reverse order.
So, what we put in first, will come out last.
In the same manner,
 it is so in the process of creation.
The absolute conscious blissful existence and it's potentiality.
So, first absolute reality.
Second it's potentiality.
Third, the potentialities creating the body out of the 'tapovana',
fourth, in this body, various kinds of senses, organs of action, mind etc.
instruments and expressions of these instruments as experience.
These are the various components of life.
The body identification and the last thing is living as body,
creating a relative and relational world.
So, our spiritual practice will be,
first, getting freedom from the relational world,
what we call as the field of 'mamata',
field of 'my ness'.
After we withdraw the 'mamata' from the world,
second stage is, 'mamata' that is 'I ness' with the body.
Freedom from 'mamata' of the world is attained by keeping away from the world.
Freedom from 'mamata' of the body is attained by self discipline and 'yogabhyasa'.
When we remain self disciplined,
we can conquer 'alasya, nidra and pramad'.
Then when the 'my ness' or possessiveness of the body is reduced,
then we come on the seat of meditation.
Relax the body.

Let Meditation Happen

Relax.

Try to recognize our existence as independent of the body.

Merely body dis-identification is not enough.

Body dis-identification also happens in dream, sleep and under medication.

We are not talking about that.

Body dis-identification plus the discovery of the presence which is independent of the body.

It is here, that 'Yoga' and 'Vedanta' differ.

In the 'viveka khyati', perfect dis-identification between 'purusha' and 'prakruti' takes place.

But, the 'purusha' does not recognize himself as the non-dual absolute reality.

On the contrary,

one among millions of the 'purusha's.

And thus the otherness and limitation born out of otherness, which are the cause for 'samsara', remain.

Hence, when body dis-identification is happening,

We should not concentrate on them but remain aware,

How in one conscious space,

manyness is created.

Out of many 'upadhis' many conditionings, many bodies are created.

Like one space, because of many pots,

is referred to as many pot spaces.

In the same manner, one conscious existence,

because of many bodies,

as if has become many.

This recognition cannot be taken for granted.

✦✦✦

MEDITATION 44

The 'purusha' and the 'prakruti',
when they are apart,
in other words,
when 'purusha' although in the company of 'prakruti', does not get influenced or identified with the 'prakruti', the 'samsara' disappears.
Identification with anything is superimposition of that thing,
along with it's modification on our being.
So, when the 'purusha', gets identified with the modification of the mind as misery,
the misery aspect of the 'prakruti', the 'chitta', the mind and the conscious existence aspect of the 'purusha', come together.
'Prakruti' is inert.
'Purusha' is consciousness.
Identification results in the inert modifications of the mind as misery.
They as if become enlivened through identification.
And a third party is born, that 'I' is miserable.
This third entity is non existing appearance.
It is this non existing appearance which undergoes the birth and death according to the 'sankhya',
but, when it is merely an appearance,
how can an appearance have a life history?
Mirage waters are appearing from time unknown.
That does not mean that they have a history.
Hence, the 'yama and niyama sadhana' in yoga, is working on the mind,
in such a manner that the mind does not undergo modifications.
When the mind doesn't undergo modification,
the 'purusha' has little or nothing to identify with.
Then knowledge becomes brighter.
As knowledge becomes brighter,

the 'viveka khyati', clear cut differentiation between 'purusha' and 'prakruti' happens.

This 'viveka khyati' is practiced, nurtured, developed through the following stages.

One, when we are living in this world,
we stop reacting,
No comments,
No appreciation,
No labeling,
No evaluation,
No condemning.
Then, how do we live?
By learning from every interaction.

Because identification means giving something a status of reality and that something borrows the status of reality from the conscious existence.

We move in this world, but, indifferent to the world.
Second technique of having 'viveka khyati' is,
not bringing the past in the present.
Third, no more worrying about the future.
But, everyday spend more time in practice of indifference to all the thoughts on the seat of meditation.

✦ ✦ ✦

MEDITATION 45

Changing the angle of our vision and position,
and thereafter looking at the same world,
gives us a different experience.
It is something like, how the city or earth looks like from an aeroplane.
What is the language we will use?
Cars and buses look like small ants running in a row.
That does not mean that cars and buses are living beings.
But, it is just an attempt to communicate to us in a language that we can understand.
In the same manner,
presently, we are caught up at the level of effect.
The body.
So, from the body identification,
when we look at the world and ourselves,
there is bound to be a sense of otherness
and also the sense of finite being.
So, when the sense of finite being and otherness is operating,
desire, anger and fear are bound to be.
With desire, anger and fear there cannot be freedom from action and 'karma'.
Hence, meditation is retake of our experiences in the same world,
where we have been living,
and are living from the cause point of view.
At this stage, it is from the effect point of view.
It is something like,
living as a wave is like living like an effect point of view.
And living like an ocean is from the cause point of view.
What seems like a great calamity for the wave,
does not have even existence in the ocean.
Such as birth, growth modification, competition and annihilation

is the story of the wave.
　For the ocean,
　　neither the wave, nor her story has any meaning.
　For the wave, it is death.
　For the ocean, it is neither birth nor death.
　Hence, living as the mind,
　　we transcend senses.
　Living as 'jiva',
　　we transcend body
　　and living as conscious existence,
　　we transcend waking, dream and deep sleep.
　Our conscious effort to move from the objects to the senses,
　　from the senses to the mind,
　　from the mind to the consciousness,
　　is the timeless, spaceless, journey to the Self.
　This journey is only of recognition.
　Now, what is that journey?
　The senses are neither attached nor influenced by the sense objects.
　The mind is neither attached nor influenced by the senses.
　The consciousness is neither attached nor influenced by the four expressions of the mind.
　Waking, dream, deep sleep and samadhi.
　This conscious existence is beyond the language of consciousness versus inertness,
　　and existence versus absence.
　Breathe a little deeper.
　Slowly move your toes and fingers.
　Offer everything to the lord.

✦ ✦ ✦

MEDITATION 46

When the hold of the mind on the body becomes loose, and the mind slowly starts going formless, as if the body is dropped, unclaimed.

As a result, only one aspect of the mind remains functional, and that aspect of the mind is inner controller, 'antaryami'.

This inner controller aspect of the mind does not create any individuality nor separateness from others.

This aspect of the mind is common for total creation, and this inner controller aspect of the mind is functional all the time.

The moment this 'antaryami' aspect of the mind ceases, the body is dropped dead.

So, there are three stages. First, inert body, where there is no life. Second stage, the body becomes capable of expressing the consciousness as mind, that enlivens the body. So, enlivened body has inert as well as the enlivened aspect.

Now, the third stage, this mind which has enlivened the body, takes the shape of the body. This shape of the mind, according to the particular body, creates separateness from others, Thereby creating an individuality, 'I' versus 'not I'.

It is this aspect of the mind that we work on, on the spiritual path. That working is, 'maitree, karuna, mudita, upeksha'. 'Maitree',being friendly means, although there is separateness but there are no differences, or although there are differences, there is no differentiation, like among the limbs of our body, there are differences, but there is no differentiation.

Hence, when we practice friendliness, this aspect of the mind, who has created the shape and the form, this aspect is erased. 'Karuna', as we have sincere concern for all the parts of our body, similarly, 'karuna' keeps the mind which includes everything and rejects nothing. 'Mudita', being happy in happiness of others. Helps us expand beyond individuality.

Let Meditation Happen

'Upeksha', indifference to the bad elements. Keeps our mind uninfluenced by them. The second aspect of mind which has taken a shape of the body, Which creates an illusion of 'I' versus 'Not I', this aspect of the mind is erased.

That is why we can say, meditation is a sleepless sleep, or the waking sleep. Sleep because there is no sense of otherness. Waking because we are aware of this. Hence, this practice is to remain other than the body.

So, the body has shape, 'I', does not have any shape. The body has a date of birth, 'I' does not have a date of birth. Body grows. 'I' does not grow. Body dies. Like, when the pot breaks, nothing happens to the pot space. This conscious space is our essential nature.

This whole phenomena is like, in the sound waves, there are mobile phones. Only the functional mobile phones have the capacity to catch the sound waves. And we say that the phone is working. In the same manner, in the conscious space is everybody.

And when anybody is able to catch consciousness and express it as mind, that body is enlivened. A living body.

When the phone is switched off, nothing happens to the sound waves in the space. When more phones are added, nothing happens to the sound waves. When a phone breaks, nothing happens to the sound waves. In the same manner, conscious existence is 'chidakasha', conscious space.

This infinite conscious space is the reality. This gets covered by the shape of the mind and further, by the thoughts in the mind. Hence, when thoughts are quietened, and even the sleep thought is not present, then the truth is revealed.

This clear picture, in our understanding, is 'viveka khyati'. Do not concentrate anywhere. Remain only relaxed and aware.

Relaxed and not aware is sleep. Totally relaxed to such an extent that the body is fully dropped from the mind, is awareness.

So, now we are not aware of the body, but aware of being.

✦✦✦

MEDITATION 47

When we relax the body,
in fact, we don't relax the body.
We may be thinking that we are relaxing the body,
but, in fact, we are giving up our hold on the shape and form of the body.
As we start giving up the shape and the form of the body from the mind,
the mind is as if freed from the prison of body shape.
Like, an ice-cube, when it is put in normal water,
slowly it starts giving up it's shape.
And the original status of formless knowledge is attained.
Earlier, the ice-cube was separately identified from the water,
although it is nothing but water.
In the same manner,
Although the mind is nothing but consciousness,
it takes the shape of the body and becomes 'jiva'.
So, consciousness expressing with the limitation of gross body identification,
becomes the mind, as waker.
Consciousness identified with the modifications of the mind becomes the dreamer,
and so on.
So, we have to go through these three operations.
First, freedom from waker,
from dreamer, from deep sleep and from samadhi purusha.
Freedom from waker is attained by body relaxation where we drop body identification.
The dreamer is dropped when we remain witness of all the thoughts and do not participate or react to any one of them.
We give up identification with the thought of absence, the 'prajnya', the deep sleep,

by remaining alert and vigilant,
that when the waker and dreamer are dropped,
but the sleep has not yet started.
But, at the same time, there is no influence of relative existence,
like that of the waker and the dreamer.
This itself is samadhi.
But, the limitation of samadhi is,
it has a beginning and end, conditioned by time.
Therefore, the first step is to attain freedom from efforts,
proper posture,
the center of gravity exactly in the center.
As we are able to relax more and more,
and our body identification is reduced,
the gross world may be perceived,
but, it doesn't disturb us.
Now, the second step is to discover freedom from the dreamer.
Instead of the mind becoming entangled in small little things,
let us do contemplation on the infinite.
To give the data of infinite to the mind,
one of the techniques is,
to subject it to the exposure of absence.
Absence of sound.
The sound begins in time and ends.
Silence is 'ananta'.
When we become more and more aware of the silence,
even those sounds which we were not hearing earlier,
they become conspicuous and no sound disturbs us.
Recognition of silence is 'ananta samapti'.
So, the dreamer is transcended.
This utter silence,
should not initiate sleep.
So, we become consciously aware and vigilant of our own being.
Now, at this stage,
we are just being and hearing is going on.

MEDITATION 48

Whatever we give importance to,
that alone enters our mind.

That which enters our mind alone becomes the source of disturbance, in the form of a seed which produces the crop of thoughts.

Thereafter the crop of thoughts becomes so wild, that the earth, the bhoomi, gets fully covered.

Then what we see is only the crop of thoughts.

The more we want to prune this crop of thoughts, it becomes thicker and thicker.

Like some type of lawns, when you start they are thin and beautiful, afterwards, they grow to such an extent, it looks as if there are wrinkles below the crop carpet.

In the same manner, thoughts are able to cover our essential nature. We give maximum importance to our own body, as a result, thoughts pertaining to the body, meaning, the waking experience begins. And in this waking experience, the waker and the associated personalities, such as brother, sister, husband, wife, they cover us. The very sub-stratum of our being. And the non existing virtual 'samsara', appears to be real.

'Asuchi, anatmani, suchi, atmabuddhi'

That which is impure, is considered as pure.

That which is not the self, is taken as the self.

That which is the abode of misery, is mistaken as the source of happiness.

'Avidya' can be considered as maya or ignorance or 'adhyarupa' of Vedanta. So, in the whole evolution,

What is the basic cause?

Our giving importance to something?

If I have started smoking, I have to stop.

No one can do it on my behalf.

Let Meditation Happen

In the same manner, we have given importance to the relative world, the relative experiences, because we have given importance, they enter our mind and destroy our peace.

Hence, meditation begins with this awareness. Whenever you are disturbed, whenever there are too many thoughts, good or bad, they are because we have given importance to something.

If something has entered our system, we have to discover the negative aspects of that thing.

Then only can we get rid of it.

This process, helps in quietening the mind.

Then, the second step.

What is the self?

What is 'not self'?

That which cannot be discarded is the self.

That which can be discarded is the 'not self'.

Keeping this equation in mind, if we work on it, we are practicing meditation.

Now, find out your self.

What is that which we discard?

Just initiate it and do it.

Anything or a person in this world, is not in the sensible former existence, any place, any product, they can be discarded and we do it.

So, in this manner, slowly find out and you will come to know, that the whole waking, dream, deep sleep and samadhi, all of them are discarded some time or the other, but, their common illuminator is ever the same. Recognition of this, is practice of meditation.

✦ ✦ ✦

MEDITATION 49

The mechanical and default approach to life is,
either we complain or we suffer.
But, the spiritual approach to life is,
we neither complain nor we suffer.
Rather, we investigate, inquire,
and thus develop this faculty, of inquiry of our own experiences.
Then, there is nothing to complain or worry about.
So, if we have some physical problem,
or metabolic problem,
simply worrying or complaining is not the solution.
We investigate,
why do I have a stomach problem?
Those who do not get into inquiry about their own food habits, digestion etc.,
they will run from one doctor to the other and things will go from bad to worse.
On the contrary,
if you become aware of what you have eaten,
what is the type of food that disturbs your digestion,
then you will be able to pinpoint the cause which will free you from the effect.
In the same manner,
Meditation is living in this awareness,
it is not a mechanical dream,
like watching TV shows and getting carried away and frustrated.
If the same thing happens on the seat of meditation,
we get carried away by our thoughts and become frustrated.
There is no difference between the two.
Hence, the first step is,
we have to be convinced in our understanding,
based on our experiences,

our interactions,
that the moment we are identified with the gross body,
the gross waking world begins.
As long as the gross body notion is valid,
till then,
the waking world will continue to persecute us.
When we drop the gross body identification,
everything is over.
Hence, the goal of meditation is,
attainment of dis-identification from the body.
So, when we sit in the seat properly,
the asana is fixed.
There is no more movement with the posture.
All efforts to sit properly withdrawn.
The third thing is,
merging in the infinite.
For this, we consciously relax the body from the top to the toes.
Starting from the head, go down, part by part,
head, forehead, eyebrows, eyes,
go down yourself.
When we have completed body relaxation,
the correctness is established, when the position has three qualities.
Firm at the base.
Vertically steady.
And the weight of the body has increased on the base of the spine or tail bone.
So, how to give the final touch?
You have to, as though, walk out of the body.
Like many bodies here in the hall, there is one which we claim to be ours.
Take a look at your own body,
from outside.
See how it looks from the front.
Relax some patches of tension if they are present.

Let Meditation Happen

Take a view from the top to the base.
Always remember,
you are outside the body.
Go to the right side of the body and take the right view.
Do this with the back and the left side too.
If we were perfect in relaxation and being observant of the body as something other than us,
the body identification will have reduced to a great extent.
The concept inside and outside the body is not valid.
Like a pot with many holes,
when submerged in the water,
the concept that the water is inside the pot or outside the pot,
is meaningless.
It is the other way round.
The pot is inside the water.
In the same manner,
we are neither inside the body nor outside the body,
but, this conscious existence is the one in which the body is.
This infinite conscious existence is the ultimate reality.
As the clouds come in the sky and disappear,
so, too, with the same momentum,
some thoughts may appear on the sky of consciousness and disappear.
This conscious space,
recognition, is 'ananta samaptidham'.
Move your toes and fingers, slowly.
Offer everything to the Lord.

✦ ✦ ✦

MEDITATION 50

When rivers are flowing, if there is some rock or something in the path of the flow, the ebbing of the water around the rock takes place.

Otherwise the water flows in one direction to reach the destination. In the same manner, the flow of life is to reach the ocean of bliss. But, when there are some rocks on the way, the flow of life starts ebbing around those rocks.

The first rock is, our gross body. The remaining rocks are, the total gross world. As long as we are identified with our body, we cannot stop thinking. Habitual thinking, called 'manoraj'.

How long can we keep chanting Lords name?

How long can we keep reading?

Because the basic error or basic cause is not removed.

Hence, the importance of 'yogabhyasa'.

And in that we also have 'ishwara pranidhan'.

By the grace of the Lord. But, that only comes to those, who put efforts. Hence, 'yama, niyama, asana, pranayama, pratyahara, dharana, dhyana, samadhi'. These are the eight essential steps. 'Dharana, dhyana and samadhi' together constitute saiyyama. Start from 'yama' and enter 'samyama'.

Hence, for living more and more in awareness, one of the simplest methods is to remain aware of one's own breathing. By this, what happens is, we are withdrawn from the past and also the future. Because we cannot breathe in the past or the future.

Breathing is always in the present.

Hence, remaining aware of breathing, and not concentrating on breathing. To become aware, if one is not used to being aware of things, for that purpose, you may increase the breathing depth and go extremely slow. Try this out a few times. Once you recognize the breathing, then step by step, you yourself will discover what is next. First our breathing was deep.

Let Meditation Happen

Then it became steady, firm, fully relaxed. Now, the breathing is slow and shallow. Now be aware of this and repeat it again.

Don't concentrate. In concentration, we give importance to the object. In being aware of something, we remain with our own self. Now, our breathing has become extremely slow and shallow.

As if the air is moving only in the nostrils, not going beyond the nostrils. Now come to all the cells of your body as a whole. The whole body expands few microns when we breathe in. And contracts when we breathe out. This expansion and contraction of the body, is because of the movement of consciousness called as 'spandana'. It is this consciousness by it's own nature, which expands and contracts. Because of this, the breathing begins.

Now, we are just aware.

Not aware of anything in particular.

Objectless awareness.

Breathe deeper.

Slowly.

Move your toes and fingers.

See the process of again identifying with the body.

The relative world begins.

This is repeated 'n' number of times.

We identify with the gross body, 'Samsara', begins. We dis-identify, but the mind keeps on projecting, dream begins.

With gross body dis-identification and freedom from thought formation, then only absolute consciousness remains.

There is nothing to be done in this.

Only recognize.

Therefore, meditation is never done.

Only remain aware. If thoughts come, go to the root of the thought and you will discover that you had become somebody.

Thus, the whole life is lived in utter awareness. Suddenly, like a bud opening into a whole flower, spiritual enfoldment takes place.

✦✦✦

MEDITATION 51

If the mind is awake, it starts running in time, place and objects.

When it starts running, 'samsara' begins.

If we enfold the mind fully, then we cannot function in this world.

If the mind is manifest, unfolded 'samsara', begins, So, presence of mind is a problem and absence of mind is a limitation.

So, we have to find out a third option, so that the mind is neither a problem nor a limitation.

Hence, 'dharana, dhyana, samadhi', When these three things are operating simultaneously, mind is manifest but it is not a limitation or liability.

It is an asset. Hence, there are certain basic things about spiritual practice, if we apply them in our lives, spiritual enfoldment starts happening. When we get up from deep sleep, in a quieter disposition, we have not yet become anybody in this world, we are still Mr. Nobody.

These basic things of the morning, toilet etc. may be completed, and before becoming anybody, before getting involved in the world, is the time for our meeting with ourselves. As Mr. Nobody. That time, depending upon the quality of our mind, if the mind is too agitated, then one should take to 'pranayama'.

That reduces agitation.

Or one can do some physical puja of the lord.

If the mind is not much agitated, But not absolutely quiet also, then we can take up chanting of the 'stotras', like, 'Rama raksha stotra', 'vishnu sahastram stotra'.

By mere chanting even if we don't understand the meaning, the mechanical chanting of the Sanskrit shlokas, has a tremendous power on quietening the mind further.

When the mind has become sufficiently quiet, then drop everything and sit. And now no more business with the mind. So, remain aware of the breathing that is going on.

Let Meditation Happen

Now and then, the thoughts will visit.

Because the mind doesn't want to die.

So, let's be vigilant, so that we are not taken for a ride by the mind or thoughts.

Hence, keep aware of breathing.

The air enters the nostrils and slowly goes upto the sternum.

The spiritual heart where the ribs join.

This column of air, from the nostrils to sternum, is only a very weak throb. So, when the breathing is the object, 'Dhyana' in one place, the heart, for a longer time, there, as if the meditation disappears.

Only breathing is happening.

This is 'dharana, dhyana and samadhi', together.

The second samadhi we studied was, 'samprajnat samadhi', where there is a clear discrimination between the moving changing matter and unchanging 'kutastha purusha'.

Unchanging means 'kutastha'.

'Purusha', the consciousness.

Thus, in 'dharana, dhyana, samadhi', the object of meditation is important, in 'sampragjnat samadhi'.

The clear understanding and their separation between consciousness, the unchanging principle, and mind, the changing principle.

Now, the third samadhi is 'asamprajnat samadhi'.

Here, the last traces of mind are dissolved.

Hence, 'asamprajnat', no relative perception, only the consciousness.

Take a deep breath.

Move your toes and fingers.

Feel as if the body is becoming real, feel the sense of otherness with the world. Sense of limited existence with your self. 'Samsara' begins.

✦ ✦ ✦

MEDITATION 52

The sequence in which the creation is explained,
in the opposite sequence, it is called, 'layaprakriya'.
The process of absorbtion.
and if we follow the steps perfectly,
slowly we withdraw from the many, and end up in the one.
The process of creation is this absolute reality,
is one without a second,
in which there is neither the sense of otherness nor the sense of limitation,
nor the sense of distantness.
The world,
the soul, the I,
the God.
In absolute reality, these mutually dependent variables are nowhere.
Now, this absolute reality has it's own potentiality and this potentiality is called as 'chetanashakti'.
Consciousness, 'avyakta, maya or prakruti'.
Now, this divine potentiality, to refer to by one word cannot be called as separate from the absolute.
Because, it is dependent on this absolute reality.
It cannot be called as one with the absolute.
Because it is referred by another name, with reference to it's effects, it is.
With reference to it's existence, it is not.
Hence, this potentiality, is as well as is not.
When we refer to 'paramatma', with reference to this potentiality,
and the potentiality remains unmanifest,
then this absolute reality 'parabrahma paramatma', is called as 'ishwara'.
This unmanifest potentiality in the next step becomes ready for manifestation,

like the seed is swollen, having been kept in water overnight.

That state is called 'mahashakti' and 'parabrahma paramatma' is called as 'hiranya garbha or sutratma'.

Now, the same potentiality has manifested into subtle and gross multiplicity,

which includes the instruments of perception and action.

The power behind them.

The instrument of knowledge and the world, which is experienced, and the gross bodies.

At this stage, 'paramatma', is called as 'vaishva nara' and the 'prakruti' is called as 'virat'.

The next step, through every body the potentiality, the consciousness,

expresses as mind and 'prana',

through the senses experiences are gathered.

And the scavenger collecting experiences is called 'jiva',

who is identified with the body, the senses, the 'prana', and so on.

Now, the meditation will be going back in exactly the opposite sequence.

So, we drop the world, come to senses.

Drop the senses, come to the mind.

Drop the mind, come to the intellect, where consciousness is reflected as 'chidabhasa'.

Now, this 'jiva', having dropped the extroverted approach to life, now, is ready to face, his own source.

Like, the reflection in the mirror is seeing the original face,

then when this ego, I, 'ahamkara', forces it's attention to it's own source,

it merges back in absolute consciousness.

Breathe deeper.

Move your toes and fingers.

Feel the body.

✦✦✦

MEDITATION 53

The knowledge where the tinge of objectivity is removed, means the knowledge where knowing and being is one with consciousness.

Hence, objectivity has to be completely erased. This objectivity in our knowledge is erased in two ways.

First, by understanding, that objectivity of names and forms is an illusion, like the mirage waters.

And second, the objectivity is essentially the same existence which has taken on the position of seer or the knower.

When the known aspect of names and forms is deleted, the knower aspect of 'I know', also gets washed away.

Then what remains is, only pure knowledge, which is not opposed to ignorance. This conscious existence is our essential nature.

So, 'May my mind merge in Rama'.

Rama means everyone remains in which and where everyone remains, is bliss. So, Rama is none other than our blissful self.

'O Lord Rama, please lift me from the objectivity'.

So our efforts must be recognized as incomplete and then, 'ishwarapranidhan', 'samadhi sidhihi', and all our efforts are surrendered at the feet of the Lord. Thus, effort putting agency, merges in the destination, the goal. Like, the one putting efforts to go to sleep, ultimately, surrenders to the sleep, sleep overpowers and the effort disappears.

In the same manner, we withdraw from the world, And in a cheerful, relaxed but urgent, inspired mood, we come to the seat of meditation. Then we take the position of Mr. Nobody. The total past is dropped. We don't decide what we will do after meditation. So, future is closed. The best way to remain in the present is to be aware of the breathing. This awareness of breathing should be as accurate and complete as while we count the currency notes!

✦✦✦

MEDITATION 54

After having completed 'yama, niyama, asana, pranayama, pratyahara, dharana, dhyana, samadhi and trayamekatra samyama',
these harvesting of the mental energy, where do we apply?

So much of efforts. So much of commitment. And after having achieved, what do we do with this?

So, those who are extrovert, they get involved in invocation of various powers within them, and then become powerful.

There is nobody who can be the most powerful in this world.

There is always comparison and competition.

As a result, the 'samsara', and relativity is maintained.

Hence, after having attained 'samyama', let us apply this energy,
not in the material world, through concentration, but, to the absolute consciousness, where we belong.

On the path of 'samadhi', these powers, 'siddhis', are obstacles and those who are extrovert, for them, these are called as 'siddhis', great divine powers.

Hence, without the 'aparvairagya', there cannot be purification of the mind.

After the mind is sufficiently purified, then the 'viveka khyati', takes place.

Intellectual appreciation of the 'purusha' to be separate from the 'buddhi or prakruti'.

Then the next step is, in this 'buddhi' we clearly recognize the objective aspect, the general knowledge about things and the reflection of consciousness as 'chidabhasa'.

So, it is this reflected consciousness or the Self identified with the thought, is the experiencer, not the absolute consciousness.

The absolute consciousness is merely an illuminator. Once this is recognized, then we remain in awareness that we don't identify ourself with the reflected consciousness in the thought.

But, only the illuminating consciousness.

MEDITATION 55

Either we are absolute conscious existence expressing through the 'panchakoshas',

or we are the expression of the absolute consciousness through the limitation of the 'panchakoshas'.

Meaning, either we are the original face or we are the reflection of our face, in water.

If we take ourselves to be the reflection in the water, then the disturbances,

the quality of the water,

will appear to have an influence on our existence.

If the water is dirty,

we will be dirty.

If water is agitated, we will be agitated.

If water is quiet, we will be quiet, undisturbed.

Thus, we will be all the time dependent on the quality of the water.

Similarly, when we take ourselves to be the reflection of the consciousness,

in the 'prakruti', the 'buddhi tattva', then we are caught up in 'panchakoshas'.

All the time we have to keep cleaning, purifying.

This we may do, but the basic problem, error, is still there,

because as many buckets of water, so many reflections.

Similarly, as many bundles of 'panchakoshas', so many will be the individualities.

Thus, we face two problems.

One with ourselves, in regard to the quality of the mind etc..

And the other problem is the sense of otherness with other reflections.

These together constitute 'samsara'.

So, when we take ourselves to be the reflection in the mind,

then our struggle will be to control and conquer the mind.
But, the basic error being the same, intact,
we will start invoking the divine potentialities in us with this newly discovered tool called as 'samyama'.
Then the new 'samsara', begins.
Like the life before and after marriage.
So, our life before we conquer 'prakruti' and afterwards.
There is no end to it.
Now, the other option left was,
we don't take ourselves to be the reflection in the mind or the thought,
but, we accept ourselves to be absolute conscious existence,
which is independent of the 'panchakoshas',
and which is freely expressing through all the 'panchakoshas'.
This is achieved through 'viveka khyati'.
Discrimination between 'purusha' and the 'buddhi tattva',
and when we correctly identify ourselves with this conscious blissful existence,
the 'samsara' and relativity is merely an appearance.
Appearance means, which appears, but doesn't exist.
Like ornaments appear on gold.
Therefore, any name and form have zero impact on the gold.
Similarly, this absolute conscious existence,
remains untouched.
By the waker,
Waking experience,
Waking world,
Dreamer,
Dream experience,
Dream world.
Tat tvam asi.
That thou art.

✦ ✦ ✦

MEDITATION 56

Today, we will chant a mantra.

Repeat it a few times and after it is over, what must happen and what happens. Thus, we get into what must happen.

In this chanting process, we will be chanting one mantra for sometime. The initial purpose of chanting the mantra is to collect the mind from all preoccupations and bring it to the cause of meditation. So, after this initial aspect is over, the mind will not be thinking much about the world.

After we have collected ourselves sufficiently, then we will focus attention on one important observation, that when we are chanting, one after another name of the Lord, is it the same mantra which concluded and again the same mantra came up, or the mantra is going on in one window and the thoughts are going on in another window?

This will be the second observation and our effort will be to close down all other windows. After this is achieved, the third step will be, we will remain aware and just be observant that the mantra begins, stays for some time and ends.

But, we, the witness, are the same.

There is no beginning, no end.

And the last observation will be, when the gap between the two mantras is widened, in that absence of mantra chanting, that which is present, is the truth. Not even the witness.

Because, witness is with reference to something other.

In this absolute presence, there is no trace of otherness.

So, these are observations. We begin from activity, chanting, controlling 'prakruti', getting out of 'prakruti' and coming to self awareness. And then, thereafter, just being.

So, let us chant slowly and steadily, no hurry.

OM SHRI RAM, JAY RAM, JAY JAY RAM. Let us chant 25 to 30 times.

MEDITATION 57

From the 'prakruti' the 'mahattattva' manifests.
From the 'mahattattva' the 'asmita'.
From the 'asmita' the eleven 'indriyas' and the five 'tanmatras'.
From the five 'tanmatras' the five grossified elements.
From these five grossified elements all the bodies of all the beings are created.
After having created these bodies,
what for and for whom are these bodies created?
For the 'bhoga' and 'apavarga' of the 'purusha'.
'Bhoga', is gathering experiences and 'apavarga' is freedom from these experiences.
Hence, the 'purusha' gets reflected in the 'prakruti'.
At this stage,
we have to be extremely careful to understand,
'Prakruti' cannot exist independently.
'Prakruti' or divine potentiality is 'brahma shraya',
is dependent on this conscious blissful reality.
Hence, this 'prakruti' cannot have any impact on 'purusha'.
Like, the depth of the ocean cannot harm the water,
or the sweetness of the sugar does not create problems for the sugarcane.
In the same manner,
this potentiality of the absolute cannot create any bondage for the 'purusha',
Then for whom is the 'samsara' and the bondage?
When 'purusha' expresses through anybody as mind,
that body gets enlivened.
In this 'buddhi tattva' 'chidabhasa', the reflection of this consciousness, creates the notion of 'I ness'.
Thus, the life is manifested in the inert body
and the conditioned expression of the consciousness is manifested

in the mind, the 'buddhi vritti'.
So, as long as there is a mirror,
there is bound to be a reflection.
In the same manner, as long as there is a thought,
there is bound to be a 'chidabhasa', the reflection of the consciousness,
and the 'jiva bhava' will continue.
When we remove the mirror,
no reflection.
Zero thoughts,
which is equal to consciousness,
there cannot be 'chidabhasa'.
and the imaginary bondage for an imaginary I disappears.
Hence, either we give importance to thoughts or we remain indifferent to them.
Let the mirror remain.
We need not look into the mirror.
In the same way,
let there be thoughts
and reflection of the consciousness in thoughts.
We need not worry about it.
This indifference, this witness, this 'sakshi', is ever the same.

✦ ✦ ✦

MEDITATION 58

Janma, Mantra, Aushadhi, Tapa, Samadhi'.

These are the five possible methods by which one can attain various siddhis.

But, it is only the samadhi which is distinctly superior to the others.

Because, for the attainment of the siddhis through samadhi,

the seeker has to get rid of the 'panchakoshas' and the 'karmashaya', etc..

So that, his mind reaches the state of 'viveka khyati', and ultimately he can recognize himself to be the 'purusha tattva'.

And the 'buddhi tattva', having fulfilled 'bhoga apavarga'.

For the purusha becomes fulfilled and goes back to it's source, prakruti.

Hence, it is necessary to understand the importance of freedom from the panchakoshas,

'Avidya, asmita, raga, dwesha, abhinivesha'.

Thus, when the seeker has sufficient dispassion for the world, then his energy which was misdirected, is conserved and is now available for application, to contemplate on the self.

This contemplation is in terms of our own experiences.

We have two sets of experiences,

one set is temporary,

where every experience begins,

remains for some time, and ends.

The second experience is a continuous experience which neither has a beginning nor an end.

So, when we are sitting quiet,

now, we are fully settled on the seat,

because of sufficient dispassion,

nothing attracts us from the world.

The mind is free.

Let Meditation Happen

This mind is now employed in discrimination between these two sets of experiences.
Every sound that we hear,
begins, remains for some time and disappears.
Then the second, third and fourth sound.
But, there is one continuous presence,
which supports the sound,
but, itself is silent.
The silent supporter of the sound is reality.
When we give too much importance to the sound,
then we get disturbed by the sound.
When we give too much importance to silence,
we are longing for silence.
The net result is that we are disturbed because of the presence of sound,
and our longing for silence, makes us more miserable,
because silence is not available all the time.
Having understood this clearly,
now we come to the eternal presence,
which is neither distorted by sound,
nor improved by silence.
This is that.
Now that we have learnt this process,
apply it and just be.

✦✦✦

MEDITATION 59

There are four options when we live in this world.

One, those who are bad people, they are engaged in criminal activity.

Two, those who are not bad, but they are dependant on everything outside themselves. When we are dependant on outside our own selves, then there will be an admixture of karma, 'Krishna and shukla'. So, either we will give in charity, salute, respect, or we will snatch away, disrespect.

Either we will be chanting the Lords name, or thinking about all other things. These kind of karmas which involve something outside, create an admixture of sin and merit. Then, the third kind of people are engaged in their own 'yogabhyasa, tapas, swadhyaya and dhyana'. In 'tapas', we do not allow the world to influence us.

In 'swadhyaya', we live our life in extreme alertness, study scriptures, and we are committed in 'dhyana'. These kind of karmas, lead to merit, 'punya karma', 'shukla karma'. So, the lowest category is 'krishna karma', then 'krishna- shukla karma', Then, 'shukla karma'. First bad, Then mixture of good and bad, Then, good. The fourth category is going beyond good and bad.

Going beyond good and bad is possible, when there is no doership involved in our life.

Doership is for the 'chidabhasa', consciousness expressing through the limitation of 'vijnayanamaya kosha', as this doership.

If there is doership, there is bound to be good or bad.

Hence, the actions in the last category, cannot even be called as 'karma', because one has transcended the doership.

So, in these four categories, the first ones are not even thinking about work. They are not walking the spiritual path at all.

Second ones are extremely dependant on the whole world.

Thereby creating friends and enemies. Thereby, in their attempt to do good, they harm others.

Let Meditation Happen

Third category are introverts and busy in their own spiritual practice.

'Tapasvadhyaya and dhyana'.

So, we must fall at least in this third category.

Thus, we are fully committed to the self.

When one is fully committed to the self, no 'not self' is entertained.

Then alone we live in the present.

To remain in the present means, there are no thoughts.

Or we do not entertain any time, space and objects.

This can be easily attained by remaining aware of our own breathing.

We are not playing with breathing.

Let it happen as it happens.

First, we will be aware of the movement of the air, which is without any efforts.

Breathing in and breathing out is not done, it happens.

Now, from here, we go to the next step.

Now, we become aware of all the cells of the body, which are also breathing. You can experience the micro expansion of your body and contraction.

This micro expansion and contraction of body is due to the throb in consciousness.

In fact, this expansion and contraction of the whole body,

is not that of the body, but of the consciousness.

Now, we take this position.

This consciousness is our essential nature.

It is not limited to one body.

But, to all the bodies.

Like, there are many phones in sound waves.

In the same manner, in the consciousness, are all the bodies.

Just as the sound waves become manifest in the phone, as sound, similarly, the consciousness becomes manifest in every body as life.

This conscious space is our real nature.

MEDITATION 60

In only matter there is no problem.
Space does not have a problem with sound.
Air does not have a problem with movement.
Fire does not have a problem with heat, and so on.
Even only the senses have no problem.
They function in their own field.
Mind doesn't have any problem.
It keeps on thinking about whatever comes in it.
Intellect doesn't have any problem.
It goes on projecting, conceiving and imagining.
Absolute consciousness, 'purusha tattva', also doesn't have any problem.
Then, for whom is the 'samsara'?
Then, for whom is the problem of this world?
When consciousness is expressing through anybody as mind,
that mind comes in contact with any particular object, through the sense organs.
A thought is formed.
That thought is enlivened in the light of the consciousness.
And the reflection of the consciousness in that thought,
called as 'chidabhasa',
appears to have experienced joy and sorrow.
So, it is this non-existing appearance,
call it 'chidabhasa' or the 'jiva',
the individual soul, which has nothing but problems.
Like, darkness can be removed only by light,
neither by sweeping, nor by washing or fanning.
In the same manner,
our miseries which are born out of wrong notions,
can be removed only by right understanding.
It is for this right understanding,

that 'shravanam' listening is required.
But, we normally listen to something and drop it.
Like, getting a medicine but not taking it.
So, 'shravanam', what we have heard, must be reflected upon.
When we reflect, the lingering doubts about what we have heard,
they are cleaned, cleared, one by one.
Like a person addicted to external enjoyments,
has no other pursuit, other than to indulge in enjoyments.
In the same manner,
Now the seeker, seeks, wants nothing but the truth.
That is 'nidhidhyasana',
Thus, knowledge freed from doubts,
is converted into conviction.
Now the conviction has to be converted into experience.
For this experience is dhyana or meditation.
Hence, in meditation we are working directly on the mind.
Neither on the other matter, nor on the consciousness.
Then, we start analyzing our own experiences.
Rather than getting buried under the load of our experiences,
either we react to thoughts or get carried away by thoughts.
Both are creators of problems.
Hence, we engage the mind in analyzing the working of the mind.
When an object enters the mind through the senses,
in the form of an image, that is called as thought.
In this thought, consciousness is reflected.
Now the thought has got both the aspects.
Inner aspect of the reflected object and the ancient aspect of the consciousness.
There is an illusion of,
as if the mind is enlivened, live.
If there is no object, no thought.
If no thought, no reflection of consciousness.
If no reflection of consciousness, no enlivening of mind,
and we revert back to our conscious self.

Let Meditation Happen

Hence, to get rid of the thoughts,
we have to have a disciplined life.
Therefore, 'yama, niyama, asana, pranayama, pratyahara'.
Do's and don'ts.
Stability in body and action.
Remaining cheerful and no more extrovertedness.
Now, when such a student comes on the seat of meditation,
he should be aware of breathing.
There is nothing we can think, about breathing.
Breathing we do only in the present.
Hence, we start living more and more in the present,
and the mind disappears.
Take a deep breath,
slowly.
In this process, body identification happens.
Again the relative world becomes real.

✦✦✦

MEDITATION 61

During our whole days interaction with the world and ourselves,
how we live or how we have lived,
is reflected on the seat of meditation.
If our whole day had been a constant fight, or,
loneliness, frustration, with the world or ourselves,
our meditation or our sleep,
will be of a similar kind.
While living our whole day and night,
if we follow a simple principle,
of non reactionary interactions.
We must not react.
When we don't react,
we act under wisdom.
What is the wisdom?
Wisdom is, the world, the body or the mind, senses, etc.,
they are the products of prakruti.
Prakruti is that being pra kruti.
Being a very clear manifestation of effect, it will have vikriti.
The effects can be both ways.
Plus, minus.
Such as health, disease.
Remembering, forgetting.
Abilities, debilities.
Love, hatred.
Achievement, failure.
This is the way prakruti expresses.
Like day followed by night and night followed by day and so on.
Similar is the story of prakruti, matter.
The illuminator of all these changes,
the purushatattva, the consciousness,
is merely an illuminator.

Let Meditation Happen

It does not get influenced by matter or modifications in matter.
When we live with this wisdom,
we don't react in the world.
When we don't react in the world,
there will be no impression in the form of likes and dislikes,
collected on the mind.
And such a mind, which is not carrying the load of likes and dislikes,
memories, arrogance, depression,
when all these things are not as a load on the mind,
that mind is 'prasanna', cheerful.
Like travelling light.
If there is a physical load on our head,
we can and we do remove it.
If there is a load of hunger and thirst,
we satiate it.
But, the load on the mind,
being of the nature of thoughts,
that load can only be unloaded by removing the thoughts.
Then we come to know,
any thought becomes powerful by borrowing strength from us.
Because our strength has gone to the thoughts,
we become weaklings and victims to the same thought.
Hence, to remove this habit of carrying the mental load,
we have to have a holistic approach to life.
Leading a life of self-discipline.
Beginning the day earlier,
the earlier the better.
Doing regular physical exercise.
Yoga, pranayama, etc..
Regular study of the scriptures.
Listening to satsang, chanting the Lord's name.
In this manner, we do not control the mind,
but, we keep the mind occupied.

Let Meditation Happen

When you are free,
immediately take yourself to meditation.
Come to recognize, how every thought,
good or bad,
begins from a point called 'somebody'.
'Somebody' is born after identification with the gross body.
Hence, our first step on the seat of meditation,
is attainment of freedom from the gross body.
Keep the body on the seat,
in a proper way.
Firm base, vertically steady,
relax totally.
Full relaxation of the body is dropping the body from the mind.
As when the body is dropped from the mind,
there is no shape of the body in the mind.
Hence, the concept of in and out is over.
The moment the concept of in and out is over,
there is no thinking possible.
Because, thinking is based on 'I',
the one who is inside the body.
And this 'I' thinks about the one inside, not 'I' who is outside the body.
Hence, how do we know whether we are fully relaxed?
This body shape and this in and out disappears from our knowledge.
The knowledge where the concept of in and out is valid,
that knowledge is called as mind,
where this concept is not valid,
it is called consciousness.
Breathe deeply two-three times.
Observe how the body is included in the mind.
The concept of inside and outside becomes valid.
Offer everything to the Lord.
Don't make a memory of the meditation.

MEDITATION 62

A clear understanding and discrimination between the factors, namely, the mind, the consciousness and reflection of the consciousness in the mind as thought.

Further, the discrimination between the three qualities of the mind.

Whether it is under stupor of tamoguna, whether it is under the attack of rajoguna, whether it is established in satvaguna or not.

A clear understanding of these four factors, will help the seeker to correct and control, thereby transcend the limitations of the 'prakruti' of the mind.

It is something like this.

When we know the traffic rules, and when we practice them scrupulously, then we go beyond the limitations of the traffic rules. We are liberated from the limitations of the traffic rules.

In the same manner, when we know the rules of matter, rules of knowledge, and practice them, not only are we protected from them, but we also transcend them.

Therefore, a clear understanding is the foundation of spiritual life.

Not the mechanical one.

So, first about the mind.

Any object to which we give importance, becomes stronger than us, enters our mind and creates a thought for its residence.

So, mind plus entry of object in mind is called as thought.

When the object has entered the mind, the thought becomes a disturbance, because, the external object is a foreign body to the mind. Hence, the reaction of the mind, in the form of desire, anger and so on.

Third, if we are not alert and vigilant, our knowledge aspect, satvaguna, is engaged in the service of rajas and tamas. Thus, the mind becomes a means of 'bhoga', enjoyment or indulgence.

Now, the same mind becomes a means of liberation, if it is living under the patronage of 'viveka khyati'.

Let Meditation Happen

Discrimination.
Any object before it enters our mind,
we must apply a security check.
We will notice that most of the objects are never used.
When the object is removed,
rajoguna does not become activated.
Satvaguna does not become matter oriented.
This is the discrimination with reference to any gunas.
Second step, the mind with the three gunas is alert.
It gathers an enlivened status,
after it receives a reflection of the consciousness.

This reflected consciousness creates an illusion of the knower, the experiencer etc. of the object included in that particular thought.

When that thought disappears, it goes along with that particular knower, of the object.

Then the second thought and second knower.
He also disappears.
So, what happens is,
individual temporary knowers plus a continuous presence of consciousness,
together give an illusion of temporary knowers to be permanent.
Thus, the waker is born.
All the wakers over a period, put together, become 'I'.
In fact, this 'I' is virtual reality, useful but non existent.
Like the latitudes and longitudes on the globe.

When this appearance is taken to be the real, nobody can help us, and when there are no thoughts, no knower, no past, no future.
Only pure consciousness.
Hence, no more entertainment of anything or any thought.

Just be.

✦✦✦

MEDITATION 63

When we take a stand of being the absolute,
and when we take a stand of being relative,
our approach to life changes.
For example,
as Chief Minister of a state,
and Prime Minister of a country,
the difference is that the CM thinks in relation to the other states,
but, the PM thinks to include all states.
He has no biasness for or against.
Because the standpoint is different.
In the same manner, when we take the standpoint that I am the body,
my lifestyle, purpose and experiences will have one set of data.
When I take the standpoint that I am the individual soul,
then I have a second set of data.
When I take the standpoint of being absolute reality,
then there will be a third set of data.
In the first, I will look at life from the womb at one end and the tomb at the other end.
When I take the stand of being the soul, 'jiva', then I will extend my life beyond these two points.
Birth and death of the present body.
And we start living life in a different manner and quality.
When I take a stand of being absolute,
then the quality of life will not be like that of the first or the second stand point.
We all have already lived our lives as body,
we know what the experiences are like,
no explanation is required.
We also have some vague notion of being a 'jiva' or soul.
Therefore, live a life of a little cultured existence,

Let Meditation Happen

where sin and merit, past life and next life are involved.
Now, let us start the third experiment.
In this third experiment, we are not in the body,
the body is in us.
We are not the 'jiva' or the soul,
but, 'jiva', or the soul is an expression of absolute consciousness,
through the body as conditioned consciousness.
Therefore, not real.
For the first two stand points,
the platform is the 'chitta', or the mind.
In the third stand point,
we transcend the mind.
Hence, the four sets of experiments of the mind,
namely, waking, dream, deep sleep and samadhi,
they come and go.
Like the clouds come and go, in the space.
So, the cloud of waking, built up around the nucleus of gross body.
The cloud of dream, built around the nucleus of subtle body.
The cloud of deep sleep, built around the causal body.
And the cloud of samadhi, built around the 'jiva bhava'.
These clouds come and go,
but, the conscious space in which these clouds move,
remains unaffected by any of the clouds.
If we correctly take the position,
being the conscious space in which these four types of clouds appear and disappear,
we will come to know,
that we don't have to do anything.
Meditation is not doing anything.
Meditation is living.

✦✦✦

MEDITATION 64

As we have default settings in our PC's, so do we have default settings in our lives.

Default settings are those, which manifest without any thinking. Similarly, out of sheer habit, we think habitually, act habitually, speak habitually. It is not an expression of life of awareness. As a result, our personality becomes strong. And we fall victim to our own lifestyle.

Hence, for our gross body, physical exercise, yoga, service, self-discipline, these are necessary. For our changing the default settings of speech, the divine theme is brought out, like chanting the Lords name. For thinking, about not the world, not the 'I', but the absolute reality.

The effect of all these three, is changing the default settings in our minds.

Hence, our patient is the mind.

Neither the world, nor the body, nor the business. But the mind. 'Chitta malahi sansareyam'.

This kind of relativity is rooted in the mind.

Hence, the first thing that a seeker must become aware is, any perception through the mind is the perception of the images. Not the reality. Like in the mirror, we see the images.

It may look perfectly like the original face, it may be useful, yet it is not the original. Similarly, whatever we know, see, is only image, and may be useful, but not real. Therefore, the thought free experience is to be recognized.

How do we know that we are in the thought free experience?

When our experience does not have the three parameters, then it is a thought free experience. Parameters of time, space and object.

✦ ✦ ✦

MEDITATION 65

A living master is like an expert driver.
A living master is like an expert actor.
The expert driver, uses the vehicle,
without getting influenced or carried away by the vehicle.
He keeps the vehicle in a fit condition, because he knows he has to use it.
So, he functions through the vehicle,
but never ever thinks that he IS the vehicle.
But, he always lives like a master.
Every small little knob, every sound, is known to him.
While driving the car,
if any door is not properly closed,
he immediately recognizes it.
So, not only is he expert in driving, but he is alert and vigilant.
About every small little thing about the vehicle.
Yet, he never gets confused, that he is the vehicle.
Similarly, a living master lives, through the body.
Keeps the body in optimum condition.
Ever vigilant and alert about every sound that the body makes.
He knows all the knobs.
Therefore, like the driver, he never mistakes himself to be the body.
He is like an actor.
He knows this is just a drama,
be it a tragedy or a comedy.
He plays the role extremely perfectly,
as if it is really happening,
but, he is far beyond that.
There are two stages.
First, acceptance of the fact that we cannot be the body,
under any set of circumstances.
Whatever may be your present experience.

Let Meditation Happen

To convert this knowledge into experience,
again two steps are required.
One, recognition of the fact that the gross body becomes meaningful only after identification with the gross body.
Hence, the sadhana will be, utter dispassion for the gross world.
If we want to achieve body dis-identification.
Second, while on the seat of meditation,
do this practice.
If I am someone other than the body, what does it mean?
Is this just a sentence without a meaning?
Thus, we want to implement this conviction to convert it into experience.
Like we imagine now, that we are inside the body,
let us imagine the other way.
Also, if we are other than the body,
why are we inside, we are outside the body.
Then the body becomes an object of knowledge.
And as the body is firm, steady and relaxed,
slowly the form of the body starts vanishing from the mind.
Then the concept of inside versus outside,
disappears.

✦ ✦ ✦

MEDITATION 66

Matter is inert, which is of different degrees of purity.
Matter with predominance of tamoguna, forms the substance of the stuff.
In this matter, there is inherent quality of change.
Changes from the present state to the next.
That is the rajoguna state of matter.
The third object is the knowledge aspect,
which is the sattva aspect of the 'prakruti'.
This matter is in the consciousness, like heat is in the fire.
This consciousness, supporting the existence of matter,
expresses differently from the three different aspects of matter.
Namely, sattva, rajas and tamas.
The tamas aspect of matter,
ultimately consolidated as different body,
the change that is inevitable in every body.
And this body has the knowledge aspect also.
Because of which the functioning continues.
This knowledge aspect is the mind.
The change of status from the gross object is 'annamaya kosha',
and in the 'vijnayanamaya kosha',
consciousness expresses as the doer or agent.
Thus, matter also inert, becomes enlivened because of reflection or expression of consciousness to the 'vijnayanamaya kosha'.
Now, these are two factors.
One is pure consciousness in which everything is,
and second thing is reflection of consciousness in the 'chitta vritti'.
One is sanctioned consciousness,
the other is conditioned consciousness.
When this conditioned consciousness, recognized by us as the real one,
the pure consciousness as if gets hidden,

behind the conditioned consciousness, and the individuality begins.

In 'viveka khyati', this process happens, that we are clearly able to recognize the medium of reflection, as 'chitta vritti'.

The reflection of consciousness in the 'chitta vritti', and the pure consciousness.

When the mind has dropped the shape and the form of the body, the mind is formless, no thought,

and in that state, in the absence of the thought,

there cannot be reflection of consciousness, to produce the 'chidabhasa', reflected consciousness, or the individuality.

And consciousness is clearly recognized as other and independent of matter.

✦ ✦ ✦

MEDITATION 67

Sequence is the foundation of 'samsara'. Because of sequence, time is born. Then comes space and objects.

From these three, we start with the object, leave the world away, while we have come on the seat of meditation.

Then, form a proper posture, firm, steady and fully relaxed. We give up the last object called as our own gross body. For that, let's start consciously relaxing the body, from the top to the toe, one sequence is established.

We relax the head, forehead, eyebrows, eyeballs, nose, lips chin, face, ears, neck, shoulders, upper arms, elbows, lower arms, wrists, palms and fingers. Relax the main trunk, chest, sides, abdomen, and below up to the base sides, lower back to the tail bone, hips, thighs, knees, calves, ankles, heels and toes. Although we have created a sequence, but, with this starting from the top, concluding with the toe, we have dropped the body.

Now, there is no gross object, with which we get lost in any sequence. Now, we come to the second stage. Sequence in thoughts. If we observe, sequence in thoughts have no meaning.

One thought from here, suddenly, second thought from there, third thought about this thing or that thing. But, there is a sequence. One after the other, meaningless arrival and departure of thoughts. This old habit of the mind, is corrected by giving a disciplined sequence. So we chant the Lords name.

Om Sri Ram, Jai Ram, Jai Jai Ram.
Om Sri Ram, Jai Ram, Jai Jai Ram.
Om Sri Ram, Jai Ram, Jai Jai Ram.

The same thought which was concluded, Om Sri Ram, Jai Ram, Jai Jai Ram. Again, the same thought is allowed to erupt. In this manner, instead of random thought eruption, now, there are disciplined thought eruptions.

When we thus discipline, the sequence can be controlled.

Then we increase the gap between the two mantras.
Slowly slowly start increasing.
Om Sri Ram, Jai Ram, Jai Jai Ram.
Om Sri Ram, Jai Ram, Jai Jai Ram.
Om Sri Ram, Jai Ram, Jai Jai Ram.
Om Sri Ram, Jai Ram, Jai Jai Ram.
Om Sri Ram, Jai Ram, Jai Jai Ram.

Thus, when we start widening the gaps, the sequence becomes weak and the silence becomes strong.

But, if we don't remain alert and vigilant, then another window is opened.

So, after we finish this, now, we can come to the awareness aspect.

Sequence is always in 'prakruti'.

Because in 'prakruti', there are many components.

Awareness is only one.

Hence, no sequence possible.

So, to recognize this awareness, we may not be able to directly jump into it.

Hence, thought free sequence is taken as a support, To get into awareness.

So, now we are merely aware of the breathing.

When we are aware of breathing, the mind is no more created.

Therefore, past and future is taken care of.

Remaining aware of breathing is keeping ourselves in the present.

As a result of this awareness of breathing, it becomes extremely slow and shallow.

Then the last step is, we are not just aware of breathing, but just being.

Having come to this point, sequence vanishes.

Because unlike everything, awareness is one without a second.

Objectivity begins only in sequence.

Sequence is creation of the mind.

In awareness no sequence is possible.

✦ ✦ ✦

MEDITATION 68

After having come on the stage of meditation,
the 1st thing must strike us is we have to get rid of the gross body identification.
That is the goal.
Firstly, the body posture should be firm, steady and relaxed.
Secondly, every thought is born to somebody,
so we have to maintain the status of Mr. Nobody.
Every time we sit, we have to remind ourselves about this.
For that,
neither our past is brought in the present,
nor our present is thrown into the future.
In the present, is only today.
Only today, has no comparison.
Only in the here, there is no comparison.
Now, we go to the mind.
When our attention is on the object, 'Artha',
we go away from ourselves.
When our attention is on thoughts,
we come closer to ourselves.
When we are aware to the meeting of thoughts,
we are still closer.
When the thoughts disappear,
only silence remains.
We are extremely near but we do not know this.
Ultimately, when we come to realize that silence of sound,
no thoughts or thoughts do not make a difference to our being.
Then, slowly objectivity starts dying away
and, objectless awareness prevails.
So to work on the mind,
Either we take any random thought
and practice on disciplining the thought,

Let Meditation Happen

by repeating a mantra.

Today, let us chant a mantra

and remember these points which are bringing us closer to our inner being.

First the content, then thoughts, then knowledge, then absence of thoughts,

then awareness of thoughts and ultimately OBJECTLESS AWARENESS.

So, let us chant ' Om Sri Ram Jai Ram Jai Jai Ram' and we will slowly march towards our own self.

The purpose of this chanting is to go beyond thoughts.

Let's chant in a sing song way, as though we have all the time in the world

and not just to get a task over with!

Chant at least 10 times.

The presence of sound and absence of sound

are mutually exclusive,

but the conscious presence is common,

it does not get influenced by sound or silence.

That is our being.

Chant again 2 times.

Both the clouds of sound and silence,

they have a beginning and end.

They come and go.

But the conscious space that is,

there is no coming and going.

That is the truth.

Mantra is chanted by the mind.

Illumined by the witnessing consciousness.

When the witnessing role is also dropped,

what remains is objectless awareness.

This is that.

✦✦✦

MEDITATION 69

'Sattva purusha yohi shuddhi samya'
Sattva is our mind
Purusha is the consciousness.
Purusha the consciousness is always uncontaminated,
uninfluenced, by the conditioning of the 'panchakoshas' or their modifications.
When the body is small, it grows,
When there is healthy or diseased conditions,
of the gross body,
in and through all this,
Consciousness remains untouched.
The 'pranamayakosha' and the rest of them, remain untouched, too.
Therefore, only recognition of the fact is all that one has to do.
If this is with reference to consciousess,
the same thing holds good,
for sattva or mind.
Mind merely receives the image
of any object on its body
and this image cannot influence the mind.
Like the image of fire,
on the surface of the mirror,
does not burn the mirror.
Or the image of water on the mirror surface
does not drown the mirror.
Similarly, learning of the objective perception,
can merely influence the mind.
'Sattva purusho yohi shuddhi samya kaivalyam'
Therefore, as purusha the consciousness
is not affected by the prakruti,
and in the prakruti, what matters to us, is the mind.

and the mind also is not influenced by all that is reflected in the mind.

Both of them must be the same.

From here we take off.

Chitta or the mind is basically consciousness,

If it is not influenced by the objectivity.

The mind is influenced by objectivity

when objective perception instead of only perception

the mind starts projection.

And if the mind doesn't project after perception, then as mind is illumined by consciousness the objective world is also illumined by the mind.

As purusha is not influenced by the minds so also the mind is not influenced by what is illumined by the mind.

Thus, objectless mind and consciousness are one.

✦ ✦ ✦

MEDITATION 70

Continuous existence,
continuous conscious existence,
continuous blissful conscious existence,
is one without a second.
We analyze all our experiences, Let it be a small experience of having a cup of tea or a comparatively stronger experience of having lunch or an even longer experience of living the day in a different place.
Every experience begins, remains, concludes.
Like we have dreamt millions of dreams,
we have also experienced many waking experiences.
They are not continuous.
They are not blissful.
Being short lived are not conscious.
They are lived through the mind.
Any experience lived through the mind is a relative experience or short lived experience.
Therefore, not a conscious blissful experience.
But, we have another kind of experience
which does not depend on the mind.
It is not the experience of anything, but, it is the experience itself.
The same beginningless, modificationless and endless experience of our conscious blissful existence.
This continuous existence and the temporary existence
is divided by a hair-thin line.
Difficult to separate like the difference between a woman and a wife!
In the same manner, we become more and more alert and dig beyond all temporary experiences.
Sounds come and go.
After the sound, silence comes, goes, And both are illumined by

that experience which has neither come nor gone.

Panchadashi told us that This conscious neither has a beginning nor an end.

It has a self limit.

All the means of knowledge, senses, mind and intelligence, they fail to know this.

To come to this awareness, we have to remain in the present. If we get locked in the past and the future, we have gone away from consciousness and we have no choice but to live in the present.

There is only one thing that happens in the present and the present only and about which we don't have to think.

So, the thoughtfree experience, in the present, is only one,
and that is our natural breathing.

We don't think and breathe.

Hence the great masters tell us to just remain aware of breathing.

No single breath should be missed.

Now take a few minutes to observe your breathing.

If we just remain aware of breathing, breath becomes slow and shallow. Now, one step further.

Breathing is not happening only in the nostrils,
but, in all the cells of the body.

Contract and expand.

So, be aware of this contraction and expansion
of the whole body at a very microscopic level.

Now, lastly, that which is contracting and expanding is the consciousness.

✦ ✦ ✦

MEDITATION 71

Summation of the finite is never equal to the infinite.
In the infinite, finite is always imagined, not real.
In the same manner, fulfillment of our desire to get happiness,
can never give us absolute or infinite bliss.
It does give us, but only a relative and temporary one.
or a passive happiness.
Passive happiness is removal of the uncomfortable situation.
First of all, we alone imagine something is important.
We alone imagine something is incomplete.
We imagine that we alone are miserable
And then we project happiness in the outer world on things and beings,
    as a result we become extremely disturbed and agitated,
    for want of that particular thing.
When we get that particular thing,
    the agitation is quietened and we imagine we are happy.
In fact, it is not happiness.
It is only absence of misery, temporarily, because then,
we project the thing again, disturbed efforts,
and the story never ends.
Hence we have to go to the cause of this.
Then we come to know
    that identification with the gross body, subtle body
    and the subsequent status of reality,
    that we give to the outer world,
    and inner world, is 'samsara'.
But, we have very clearly seen,
    we continue to exist even in dream state,
    when not identified with the gross body
    and the gross world.
We continue to exist in the deep sleep,

when not identified with the gross body
and the subtle body and the respective worlds.
We continue to exist in 'samadhi' when all the three bodies,
causal, subtle and gross are disowned.
Meaning we are independent existence.
So many bodies have come and gone,
like clouds in space.
Space is not influenced.
In the same manner, the conscious space that we are,
in this conscious space,
waking, dream, deep sleep and samadhi,
these clouds come, from nowhere.
And disappear, nowhere.
Conscious space remains the same.
Each experience in the waking, dream etc. is finite.
Summation of the finite experience is not infinite life.
Life is much more.
This conscious existence
is our experience without the medium of senses, mind or intellect.
This is what is the truth.

Therefore, the first step in spiritual practice is to come to recognize ourselves as someone different and independent of the gross body.

✦ ✦ ✦

MEDITATION 72

Waking experience is like seeing a live show on the stage of the mind.
Dream experience is like seeing the album of the show.
Waking experiences are reflections of the world on the mirror of the mind and seeing those images.
But, because we are identified with the gross body,
we take these images of the waking experiences,
as solid.
In fact, they are only images.
Similarly, in case of dreams,
these are only the replay of earlier images,
without any proper order or sequence.
Hence, instead of seeing the pictures clearly,
we see the collage.
While seeing the dream collage,
we feel it is real.
But, having given up the identification
with the projection of the mind,
they are recognized as just the pictures
or a slide show.
The difference between these two experiences is,
in case of the dream, memories are illumined
by consciousness and in the case of waking,
the images of the objects are illumined
and in that process, not only the waking experience is happening,
but the dream sequence is also subconsciously prepared.
These two experiences,
both of them are on the mind's platform,
on the screen of mind.
The difference is like a live telecast of a cricket match
and a replay.

Hence, in both cases, the illuminating 'chetan satta samvit aatma purusha,'
Conscious reality, is the same.
Like the one who has seen the live telecast
and the one who is seeing the replay in the news bulletin.
Hence, although there are three kinds of experiences
on the screen of the mind,
the illuminating consciousness is the same.
This is the original live match, telecasting,
somebody is clean bowled out,
somebody has hit a century,
In the dream we may see the same
or a mix up because order and sequence get mixed up in the dream.

Therefore when this 'viveka khyati' takes place, and we recognize our identity with the 'purusha', then we become, or discover that we are the substratum of the 'prakruti'.

Having discovered to be the total support of the prakruti,
differences on account of the conditioning, they disappear.
When the reflection of the sun on the lake seems to be broken,
To whom? To the sun, not to the reflection itself,
because reflection appears and it is not.
Similarly, the modification of the reflection of consciousness, 'chidabhasa', in the 'vritti'
appears to the pure consciousness
as if undergoing change, but to the 'chidabhasa' itself it cannot, because 'chidabhasa' is just an appearance.

✦ ✦ ✦

MEDITATION 73

When the body is included in the mind,
a part of the weight of the body,
is held in the mind
and a part is with the element earth.
Thus, our body weight is divided into two places.
The body is supported by both earth and the mind.
Thus when the mind is holding the shape, form and weight of the body,
the mind gets tired after some time and then drops the body
and we enter deep sleep experience.
When the mind drops the body,
there are no thoughts in relation to the body.
And the waking experience is discontinued.
When the same thing is consciously achieved,
it is called as 'samadhi'.
Hence, in a proper posture,
when the body is firmly seated,
vertically stable
and the whole body is dropped from the mind,
by the process of relaxation.
When we start relaxing the body
from top to the toe,
in fact, the body is not relaxed, but,
the mind drops the body's shape and form.
Then the mind merges with the total mind
and as the result of unloading of the body weight, from the mind,
the mind is free from relativity.
'shuddho dharmo vivartate'
when the mind is free from the load of relativity,
it becomes purer and purer.
And this is what is called as the

'Dharma megha samadhi'
with regular practice of releasing the mind from the body, shape and form,
the purity of the mind is in terms of experiencing the meaning of 'tatvamasi mahavakya'.
So, by the instruction of the teacher,
one although not experienced,
gets convinced that the doer is not 'me'.
Everything is happening in prakruti,
as a result,
the total accumulated 'karma' are burnt away.
When the mind has become more and more subtle,
the immediate experience of being the conscious self,
the jiva bhava, the sense of an individual soul,
that is also burnt away.
When the jiva bhava is burnt away,
then the truth remains, to be non-dual,
Conscious blissful existence.

✦ ✦ ✦

MEDITATION 74

Existence is more pervasive than anything that is cognized by us objectively because existence is not only recognized in the objects of knowledge but also recognized as ones whole being.

Thus, on ones absolute existence the objectivity and subjectivity is superimposed. This is the truth. However, instead of recognizing this existence as the substance and 'I' versus 'not I' as the superimposition on this substance, our understanding is exactly the opposite. 'I' and 'not I' they become the substance and existence becomes the attribute. Like, on the absolute existence, space is superimposed.

But our understanding is, space becomes the substance and existence becomes the attribute. In pure existence there is none other than the existence. Non-dual. Hence, the factor that creates duality, namely, space, does not exist at all in the absolute existence. By this inexplicable power 'shakti' called as 'maya', the space is projected and opposite of existence is imagined, namely, emptiness. This emptiness creates the duality of 'I' versus 'not I' and this becomes the substance and existence is the attribute.

Hence, first we become aware of breathing, so that the thinking process is not initiated. And whether breathing is in or out, awareness is continuous. There is discontinuity in the breathing in and breathing out, but, not in the awareness. This continuous awareness is the absolute truth. Initially we may be aware of breathing, but ultimately it is awareness alone!!

✦✦✦

MEDITATION 75

These bodies are subject to destruction.
When we understand destruction of the body,
normally we take into account only death
and disintegration of the five elements.
But, destruction of the body is happening
every moment.
Cells are created and destroyed.
In fact, there is no destruction.
There is a series of creation and destruction
resulting in constant change.
And this constant change is applicable only to that which is finite.
Creation is adding something.
Destruction is taking away something.
To the finite alone addition and subtraction are possible.
The second type of destruction is,
when we are not identified with the body.
Everytime we are not identified with anything finite,
that is the destruction of the finite and the liberation of the infinite.

Thus, the continuous unbroken existence, supports many bodies that come, hang around and disappear.

On this continuous existence, is superimposed the knower and the known.

The known is also superimposed on the existence,
hence it is known.

The knower also exists superimposed on the same existence.

Hence is the knower. When the knower is influenced by the known, He is a finite knower.

And when the knower is not influenced both by the known and the knower,
one has reached the correct identity.

MEDITATION 76

All the spiritual practices remain in the present.
Remaining in the present means going beyond time.
Remaining in the present means merging with the absolute.
Remaining with the present means deleting the total past, closing the possible future and going beyond the beginning and end.

The battle that we face on the stage of meditation is fighting with time. Fighting with unborn time. Hence, everything, questions, answers, achievements, failures, memories, projects, whatever we have learnt in the past, everything we drop. Water does not have present, past and future. Waves have past and future. A long past and unknown future. And the present is just for a moment. But, the truth is, present is infinite. In this infinite present, past is just a projection, illusion.

If we go back in our past, how far can we go? 70 years, 60 years, 50, 20, 10, 1. Just so long. And when we reach the womb of the mother, to the first day and before that we didn't exist. If we did, we were in another form.

Then how much backwards can we go?

We end up into the unknown, because we are knowledge And when we go away from our own selves, we end up in ignorance. Hence, remaining in the present is the only option. And only life. There is nothing that we have to achieve. Nothing that we have to protect. Yet, our old habits drag us in the past, or throw us into the future.

Hence, the mind has to be kept busy or you have to remain indifferent to the mind. If we can remain indifferent, there is nothing like that. Alternatively, be aware of breathing. Do not concentrate on breathing because we breathe only in the present.

✦ ✦ ✦

MEDITATION 77

Unless there is manifestation in the form of effect,
the unmanifest cause is not known.
In the relative world, unmanifest being the cause and manifest being the effect,
one unknowingly develops a faculty of thinking only within the matrix of cause and effect.
And when we are caught up in this net of cause and effect, we do not transcend the cause and effect,
and thus remain buried under thoughts.
As Bhagawan says in the 2nd chapter of the Bhagawad Gita,
This truth is not that it has become manifest
and then it has become unmanifest.
No, the drama of manifestation and unmanifestation, is going on, on the stage of this absolute reality.
Hence, when the mind is active, it brings in cause and effect, one way or the other.
In 'karma', it comes in the form of do good and get happiness etc…
In 'yoga', practice this, result freedom from health problems etc…
In 'devotion', invoke Him and He will come and help you.
But, when it comes to enquiry, you don't get anything.
On the contrary, on the relativity, superimposed on the substratum,
that alone is erased.
Hence, meditation will be going beyond cause and effect.
It will be going beyond mind.
To go beyond the mind, we have to transcend the mind.
We can do that if we remain in the present,
by remaining aware of our breathing.
Now, the meaning of this statement is,
we are not concentrating on breathing,
as is done in pranayam.

Let Meditation Happen

In pranayam, the mind is created and maintained.
Because efforts are there.
But, when we are just aware of breathing,
now, our position is not in breathing.
Our position is with our own self.
t is like standing in our own balcony and observing the traffic on the road.
So, the first thing to clear is,
en we remain merely aware of breathing,
we remain in the present.
reathing being a continuous process,
we remain continuously in the present.
In other words, our moment of present is lengthened.
Because we are not thinking of breathing,
so, there is no memory of breathing.
In awareness, there is no memory.
Hence, our present is not momentary,
but, a long one.
Normally, our position is in the 'sattva guna' of the meditation.
But, we are still in the 'prakruti'.
Now, our position is not in 'sattva guna' but in the awareness that we 'are'.
There is a possibility that in the 'prakruti', 'sattva' can be contaminated by 'rajas' and 'tamas'.
But, by remaining merely aware of our 'being', awareness is always the same.

✦✦✦

MEDITATION 78

The importance that we give to anything in our life, becomes our pursuit in life.

If we have given importance to wealth, we pursue that.

If for worldly indulgence, we engage in that.

If for matter, our spiritual practice remains matter oriented.

If we have given importance to 'dharma', our spiritual practice is 'dharma' oriented.

If we have given importance to devotion, devotion becomes our spiritual practice.

And, if we have given importance to absolute reality, then our approach to life changes.

Therefore, our meditation depends on what we have given importance to.

If we have accepted this principle that relativity is possible only in imagination of the absolute, then we know that relativity cannot be real.

In relative experiences, there cannot be absolute bliss.

And in the absolute being,

there are no limitations.

It constitutes all bliss, all the time, everywhere effortlessly.

From this absolute standpoint, there will not be any doubt.

Hence, we have to change our standpoint in life.

The change in the standpoint is from the absolute standpoint.

'Karma yoga', devotion and knowledge become easy.

Spiritual practice from absolute standpoint.

Just finish your duties sincerely and relax.

From yoga point of view, discriminate between 'purusha' and 'sattva', the mind.

To achieve that, quieten the mind.

From devotion point of view, everything that happens in life is His will.

Let Meditation Happen

No reaction, no retaliation. Every experience is a reminder of the Divine Plan.

From the knowledge point of view, I am not in the body or the world etc. but everything is in me. Like, the ocean does not feel the load of the waves.

Thoughts are always about others.

Like eyes can see others, never themselves.

So, we have to remain indifferent to thoughts.

Riding the vehicle of thoughts, we go away from our absolute self.

Any thought comes, no interaction, no getting involved with it.

Just when the objective thoughts reduce, the thought aspect of the 'I' also weakens.

Ultimately, thoughtfree 'I', the absolute self is revealed.

Therefore, remain aware.

In that awareness, objectivity disappears.

✦ ✦ ✦

MEDITATION 79

Whenever we become aware about something,
such as, desires, anger, that cannot hold long on us.
Hence, meditation is not a momentary short time exercise,
wherein we sit and struggle.

Rather, meditation is a poise which we achieve when the dormant divinity in us surfaces.

First, we become aware of things.

This practice of remaining aware of things, reduces the intensity of impact of those things, on our mind.

With continued persistent practice, the awareness component increases.

The objectivity from the awareness, reduces in that proportion.

Ultimately we end up in objectless awareness.

The other way, is that we do this 'bhavna',
that the Lord is observing us every moment.

Our beloved Lord, Bhagawan Krishna, is observing every thought, every word, every action, by residing in our heart.

So, as we do not behave wrongly if someone whom we respect is near about,

in the same manner, our mind etc. remain quieter with the thoughts of the Lord watching us, and that mind is then engaged in reflection.

That which was neither born, nor will die, unborn without modification and change, is the truth.

The meaning of every word thereafter will indicate our own Self.

That which was not born is our own being.

✦✦✦

MEDITATION 80

In the meditation of reality, the whole phenomena of life is looked upon from the absolute stand point.
How the world is seen by the Lord, that alone is the right vision.
Hence, the consciousness that we are, is expressing through the body, the senses, the mind, etc..
Hence, differences are created because of the conditioning of the senses and the mind.
When this conditioning is disowned, as in deep sleep,
our experience of otherness disappears.
Our experience of being a limited entity,
separate from the totality, also stands cancelled.
Hence, the only way to discover absolute bliss,
is to transcend the senses and the mind.
The senses are controlled by firm decisions and flat refusal
to indulge in worldly objects by self imposed discipline.
The mind is transcended by educating the mind.
So, when the world is kept outside and the mind is educated and given the goal,
the goal has to be clear for the mind.
Like there is one mind peeping out through many holes.
In the same manner, there is one consciousness which is peeping out through many bodies.
Just as, because of many senses, the mind appears to be many but is one.
In the same way, because of many bodies, the one consciousness appears to have become many.
This undivided, non-dual conscious experience, 'chetan satta' is ONE.
Take a deep breath.
Slowly move your toes and fingers.
Offer everything to the Lord.
Don't make a memory of the experience of meditation.

✦ ✦ ✦

MEDITATION 81

Why are names and forms called illusions?

Because, that which was not in the beginning and will not be afterwards, and only appears in between is illusion. That which cannot be denied or altered, is the truth. In every perception, there are two aspects of knowledge. One, about illusion. Second about substratum supporting the illusion. When our attention goes to the illusion, then although the substratum is supporting, it gets covered, clouded by the illusion.

So, what is the reality and what is the illusion in our experience?

Every sound that we hear, has these two aspects. Illusory and the real illusion. Every sound begins, remains and ends. Every sound is recognized as existing. This is about the object or field of experience.

What about the experiencer?

With everything known, a knower is born. Object one, knower one. Object one goes away, knower one goes away. Object two, knower two. Object two goes away, knower two goes away. But, there is a continuous existence. Because every knower exists. In this way, the illusory aspect of the object, and the illusory aspect of the experiencer of the object, are both supported by the same existence. In other words, on the absolute existence, objectively there is a superimposition of names and forms. And subjectively, superimposition of the knower. When the knower devalues the known, both the illusions disappear. And what remains, is absolute existence. Tat twam asi. That thou art. This existence is recognized as non-dual, one without a second, reality. It is possible, by being indifferent to the world, being indifferent to our experiences, and the experiencer associated with every experience.

✦✦✦

MEDITATION 82

As in the liquidity of water, fish and other lives survive, they move in water very comfortably.
As the other animals, move and live comfortably in the space, both the water and space, do not get influenced by the contents.
Similarly, mental space does not get influenced by the contents, the thoughts. The conscious space does not get influenced by the waking, dream, deep sleep and samadhi. Like the picture on the canvas looks so enchanting, full of diversities, mountains, rivers, trees, animals, human beings that cover the substratum, the canvas.
But, when we look at the picture, we don't pay any attention to the canvas, without which the picture cannot exist.
In the same manner, we give so much importance to the world, although we see the world as something and existing.
Existence get hidden behind the attributes.
The existence gets hidden behind the 'panchakoshas'.
Thereafter, names and forms become real.
Man and woman.
Young and old.
Hungry and thirsty.
Happy and miserable.
Success and failure.
All these become real.
Hence, 'apavada' means, when the names and forms of the ornament are removed, that which was supporting the name and the form, of the ornament, called as gold, that alone is real. Similarly, when the names and forms of the world and the 'panchakoshas' are denied,
what remains is 'chetan satta' the conscious existence.
Knowledge divided in the object and subject is mind.
Knowledge homogeneous, undivided is consciousness.

✦✦✦

MEDITATION 83

From that 'parabrahma', which is the self, space is created.
What is space? Nothing.
That means, there is no creation.
There is but absolute reality.
Nothing is created, means there is but one absolute existence,
and that was, is and shall be, because nothing is created.
So is the case of the mind.
So, mind also is not.
Because of the mind, concepts of time, space and objects are born.
Yet, we experience, although there is nothing.
Then, what is this?
Therefore, other than the infinite reality,
everything is an illusion.
It appears on the substratum of reality, but is not.
Like, the pot space is covered by the water space,
so also the substratum is covered by the projection.
Objectivity in projection is the world.
And subjectivity in projection is the 'jiva'.
Either we discard the appearance of the world as an illusion
and don't get influenced by them,
we are then in tune with the divine.

Or, we reject the 'jiva bhava' and allow the 'satyam', 'jnayanam', 'anantam brahma' to express through the conditioning of the body mind complex.

✦✦✦

MEDITATION 84

In the morning, we become aware of this sense of 'I',
which is ever present.
During our whole days activities, we are lost in the world.
At night, we are not aware of anything.
So, right in the beginning of the day,
we become aware of this eternal presence, first.
After we become aware of this eternal presence,
then alone, the world comes into cognition.
Now, how do I become aware of this?
This is not the 'I' that is opposed to the 'you' or 'he'.
Rather, it is conscious blissful existence, called 'turiya'.
Because it is conscious blissful existence and beyond, the fourth state.

This is a 'paramhansa gatim'. It is here that the great 'jivan mukta mahatmas' rest.

And, it is 'turiya' because it is supporting the three, the waking, dream and deep sleep.

Hence, when it is called the fourth, it does not mean, like the waking and dream cannot exist together, dream and deep sleep cannot exist together, this 'turiya' cannot exist with any one of them. No.

On this 'turiya tattva', is superimposed the 'chidabhasa', the relative 'I'.

That homogeneous, pathless, infinite called as 'brahman' is the correct meaning of 'ahama'. Not the assembly of the elements.

✦ ✦ ✦

MEDITATION 85

The one whose mind is not at ease with himself,
he cannot have proper 'viveka',
discrimination between the witnessing consciousness and the 'panchakoshas'.
He is always preoccupied with the world.
He can never get attracted, involved.
He can never get into the mood for devotion or inquiry.
At this moment, our 'bhava' is,
The world is real.
It has got a value.
'I' as the body am real.
This is our present 'bhavana'.
Such an extremely disturbed person cannot be attracted towards the truth.
He who has not fallen in love with the absolute
will keep on struggling throughout life,
for getting peace by running after the pieces.
How can a disturbed person ever be happy?
Such persons, live at the level of matter to such an extent,
that they are not aware of how much disturbance they create around them.
While walking, talking, sitting, keeping shoes, opening a book etc..
This happens when we do not live in awareness.

✦ ✦ ✦

MEDITATION 86

Having created all the bodies in His creation,
the Lord thought, 'For whom are these bodies?'
Then he entered the bodies from the top.
The entry of the absolute reality in His creation,
is like the space entering the pot and becoming pot space.

In fact, we may refer to it as space, but the total space in which the pot is created, is always existing. So, the pot space has not entered. It was already there. In the same manner, entrance of the Lord in His creation, is an entry without an entrance.

So, what does this mean?
The meaning is, when importance is given to the body,
then the 'jiva' is created.
When importance is given to the pot walls, pot space is created.
When we call it pot space, it is essentially the total space.
But we bring the pot into use and pour water into it.
A 'jalakasha' is manifested
and in that 'jalakasha', the reflection of the space in the water,
hides and covers pot space and also total space.
It is this water in the pot space that has created the problem.
So, should we not keep water in the pot?
Should we not use the pot?
In the same way, In the pot of the body is the water of the mind.
In this mind is reflected the conscious space, which hides the original space, 'chidakasha'.

When the absolute presence is not recognized behind the relative presence, when the 'kutastha chaitanya' is not recognized behind the 'chidabhasa', the 'samsara' begins.

When absolute consciousness is recognized, behind relative experience, 'samsara' ends.

✦✦✦

MEDITATION 87

When 'anandamaya kosha' is recognized as 'ishwara',
we bring the 'ishwara', the God,
very close to us.
Then, it is out of this 'anandamaya kosha' the temporary 'pralaya',
then again the waking and the dream experiences begin.
This unmanifestation and manifestation is going on incessantly.
When we take this as a natural phenomenon,
life is just lived through.
There is nobody who is living the life.
When we reach this status of 'nobody',
there cannot be any desire.
Therefore, there cannot be any 'karma' or activity born.
Therefore, no 'samsara'.

✦ ✦ ✦

MEDITATION 88

The process of superimposition and de-superimposition,
is the process of an inquiry.
What we see or experience,
is it that way,
or the other way round?
We see a picture or a painting,
is it just existing nowhere?
We go one step behind the painting,
and come to discover, before it was filled with appropriate colours,
there were only sketches and an outline. Before these there was a thin layer of starch.
That layer made it possible to draw sketches.
Is the starch staying by itself, in nowhere?
Now, we come to discover that behind the starch is the canvas.
But, normally, when we are preoccupied with the painting,
we don't even suspect the support.
As regards a painting is concerned,
it makes no difference.
But, when we see the beautiful painting of the world,
without knowing the substratum,
we are influenced by this world.
Hence, when we observe the great masters of this world,
they are happy and cheerful.
Why can't we be the same?
Such a seeker of higher vision,
when approaches a teacher,
the 'acharya' says,
"discover whether you are the body or the 'jiva', or the 'kutastha chaitanya'"
Body we cannot be, 'jiva' we mistake ourselves to be, because in fact,

'Jiva' merely appears, but is not.
On the canvas of the 'kutastha chaitanya'
is the starch of 'anandamaya kosha',
there is a picture outline of many things and beings in the form of 'samsara',
The 'tejasa' or the 'hiranyagarbha'.
When the 'jiva' gets identified with the body,
so the miseries of the relative world and the reality of the 'kutastha chatanya' get mixed up. The 'I' as a 'jiva' becomes real and miserable.
Hence, merely suspending thought formation is not the way out.
So, we take some support to get out of this relative existence.
Like the pot space and the total space.
The pot space is fully hidden behind the water space, 'jalakasha'.
In fact, when the pot space is holding water, the pot space is not touched by the water.
How can the 'jalakasha' hide the pot space?
In this way, when we take our body to be like a container,
In this container, there is a pot space
and in this pot space, are the waters of mind, in which is reflected the total space along with the contents.
We get so influenced by them, that the pot space is forgotten.
Hence, take the position of space,
and come to discover,
that our real nature is not inside the body, imprisoned,
But, the body is in us the conscious space.

✦✦✦

MEDITATION 89

No experience ever happens without the substratum of 'I'.
Where 'I' is not directly or indirectly involved,
no interest or value is given to that experience.
For example, some good event happens.
Like the birth of a child.
Now, this event is of no meaning if the 'I' is not involved, directly or indirectly.
And therefore, any discussions, anywhere, any topic, whether required or not required, the "I' is brought into the picture.
Suppose, some people are discussing about their children,
How they are good or bad,
how they have taken up the business, very efficiently, etc..
The onlookers never have an interest in them,
we may just make a passing comment that our children are very nice.
Now, there was no reference or requirement to bring our children in the discussion.
But, then, where 'I' is not, the world does not exist.
So, this is the story of the two 'I's.
'Jivas' world exists in the relative 'I'.
'Ishwaras' world in the 'ishwara's I'
'Jiva' doesn't have only one 'I'
He has dozens of them.
'I' as rich or poor, 'I' as educated or uneducated.
'I' as lucky or unlucky, man or woman.
The list is unending.
And we get lost.
As our whole life is in search of that 'I', who is absolute happiness.
So, Vedantic Sadhana is to evaluate every 'I' and see the worth of that 'I'.
Is it worth destroying our self for this temporary, flimsy 'I'?

Thus, we start reflecting, one by one, each 'I'.
Then we come to a little understanding,
That all these 'I's are based on the basic error of body identification.
Then our sadhana becomes body dis-identification.
After we are convinced of this,
then we do 'bhavana', that like space we are formless,
like space we are untouched by the gross world,
the thought world, and the waker, dreamer etc..
Like space is called the pot space and total space,
this happens because we give importance to the pot.
In fact, space alone is in and out of the pot!
In the same manner,
this conscious space alone is the reality,
and like, breaking the pot does not harm the pot space or total space,
in the same manner, the conscious space remains untouched by the gross world,
the experience of the gross world and the experiencer.
Now, this is 'bhavana'.
With this 'bhavana', as we will go firm, the shape and size of the body will disappear from our knowledge.
This homogeneous conscious existence is the reality.

✦ ✦ ✦

MEDITATION 90

There is nothing that we can do, talk about or to alter the world and relative experiences. We can improve something if it is existing.

If it is just an appearance, there is no possibility of improving the appearance.

When we thus, change our understanding, about the world,

our approach to the world and worldly problems undergoes tremendous change.

As we cannot change, improve the content of dreams,

we can only do one thing,

we can laugh at it and forget about it.

Similarly, the waking, dream, deserve only this much attention and when we drop the objective world, the objectless awareness shines forth.

This objectless awareness we cannot talk about, discuss or improve upon, because we are no more anywhere.

Dissolved in the absolute.

So, the conclusion is, about the world we can do nothing.

Because it is an appearance and not a reality.

About absolute truth also we can do nothing because we disappear.

We can have desires about something which is recognized as real.

All the desires in our heart disappear when the world is discovered to be an illusion.

Hence, correct understanding of the 'jiva', 'jagat' and 'ishwara' is the foundation of realization.

✦✦✦

MEDITATION 91

When we take this word, the 'purusha' or the 'jiva', more than the word 'jiva', the 'purusha' is appropriate.

If we have the correct understanding of the word 'jiva', then we come to know that they are synonymous.

The meaning of the word 'purusha' is, the one who is residing in the body, or the body is 'purusha'.

The one residing in the gross body is the waker.

The one residing in the subtle body is the dreamer and in the deep sleep, the 'prajanya'.

But, there is another meaning also.

That is, the one who is infinite.

Therefore, when we talk of 'jiva' or 'purusha',

we have to talk of this 'jiva' along with the 'kutastha chaitanya'.

'Kutastha chaitanya' expressing through the limitation of the gross body is called the waker.

So, for the experience of the waking world, waker is necessary.

But, this waker has no independent existence.

It is the 'kutastha chaitanya' getting manifested through the limitations of the gross body.

Therefore, incomplete expression of the 'kutastha chaitanya' is dreamer.

So, when we understand ourselves in this light, and then analyse our experiences,

that the waker, dreamer etc..are limited manifestations,

during that particular dream and waking experience.

When that dream and waking experience is over, they disappear.

Meaning, earlier they were only appearances. Not reality.

Hence, when the mirage disappears,

there is no loss of water,

because in the appearance of the mirage, there was no water.

In the same manner,

Let Meditation Happen

For every waker and dreamer,
'Kutastha chaitanya' is the substratum,
Without this, no waker and waking experience is possible.
Thus, when our attention is on this unbroken, continuous presence,
which is never denied as that of the waker and the dreamer,
we have discovered the truth.
When this fictitious identity, the 'jiva',
is recognized as a character on the stage of life,
then there will be the presence of joys and sorrows,
but there won't be a joyful or sorrowful personality born.
Thus, life is lived.
Without anybody being born this infinite 'kutastha chaitanya' is the reality.

✦ ✦ ✦

MEDITATION 92

The dream experience is gone through by two entities.
One is the one who is influenced by the dream.
And the other one only illuminates that dream,
without getting influenced by the dream.
When the dream is over,
the one who is influenced by the dream, normally the dreamer, he disappears.
And the memory of that dream is recorded on the mind,
which includes the dreamer also.
And in the waking experience again,
This memory of the dream is also illumined by the same witnessing consciousness,
which was present during the dream, but which was not influenced by the dream.
So, in the waking experience, it was a good or a bad dream.
This memory is again illumined by the witnessing consciousness and owned by the waker.
that 'I had a good or a bad dream.'
In fact, the waker was not present in the dream.
How can he have the memory of the dream?
Hence, this 'jiva', the waker, borrows the continuity of presence from the 'kutastha chaitanya', from the witnessing consciousness, the 'chetan satta',
and owns the memory of the dream,
and together says, ' I had a good or bad dream!'
So, when this waker does not hesitate to steal away the memory of something ,
where he was totally absent,
will he ever hesitate to own anything that is not his?
Such as, the body etc..
Hence, meditation is living in this awareness,

Let Meditation Happen

that in this sky of awareness, 'chidakasha', are passing a series of clouds, namely the waking, dream and so on.

This 'chidakasha' remains uninfluenced.
When the 'jiva' recognizes himself,
not as the 'chidabhasa',
not as the experiencer of the experiences,
but, merely the witnessing consciousness.
The first thing that happens as a result of this is,
desires will not be possible.
The space cannot have the desire for clouds.
When there are no desires,
life is like playing a role on the stage.
As if we are talking,
as if we love somebody,
as if we threaten somebody,
as if we suffered a lot.
But, in fact, nothing happens.

In the same manner, when one comes to discover his eternal presence, desires disappear.

Means, there are no more thought eruptions that create a reality in relativity.

But, the potentiality of thought formation is involved to play the role in the 'dharma' of life.

Breathe deeper.
Slowly move your toes and fingers.
Offer everything to the Lord.
Don't make a memory of the experience.

✦✦✦

MEDITATION 93

Every activity in our life, is for getting happiness.
This activity seeking happiness is born because we are not happy, now.
And, why are we not happy?
Because, our blissful nature is covered by a virus of desire at three places.
Senses, mind and intellect.
Hence, when we go to the satsang,
we are told that we ourselves are of the nature of bliss.
This is indirect knowledge.
Afterwards we inquire, what does it mean, that we are blissful?
It means, that we no more function in the relative realm.
In the absolute, undivided experience alone there is bliss.
Hence, we go beyond, all that is creating the relative experience.
In this manner, one goes beyond the 'buddhi'.
We give up objects.
We come to our senses.
Give up senses.
Come to the mind.
Give up mind.
Come to the intellect.
When we come to the intellect,
our dis-identification from the body and senses is complete.
Now, we are taking ourselves to be the 'jiva'.
This 'jiva' is no more allowed to think about the relative world.
Now, we are absolutely steady.
Free from all disturbances, movements, changes.

✦✦✦

MEDITATION 94

We are fully convinced that we are the body and we live that experience, every moment.
Our goal on the spiritual path is to be equally convinced that we are not the body,
and we live through the body but no more as the body.
This is the goal.
Working on the goal is working on 'Tat Twam Asi' mahavakya.
So, at this moment, our experience is far away.
Therefore, when we start inquiring according to 'Tat twam asi' mahavakya,
we have to practice the purified and correct notion of 'I'.
What does 'I' mean?
Then our scriptures tell us,
That which is not subjected to any change, any modification,
That which is without beginning and end,
That which is without form and shape,
That which is illuminating everything but does not get influenced by anything,
That is the meaning of the word 'I'.
So, when we sit for meditation,
It is on this purification that we work.
A proper seat is arranged so that we don't have to bother about the body's comfort.
A proper time is arranged so that the mind is co-operative.
After having sat in a proper place at a proper time in a proper way,
our attempt should be to park the body on the asana and forget about it.
As much as we are not identified with the body,
to that extent, we are on the right track.
Through diligent practice and educating the mind,
we separate ourselves from the gross body,

means, the 'I' is taken to be formless.
As a result,
the body will be fully relaxed,
the mind would have dropped the form of the body
and now the experience is that of bodyless existence.

The bodyless existence means nothing of the gross world has any consequence.

Like in deep sleep,
we are fully detached from the body,
in the same manner,
the basic difference is in sleep the mind goes back to 'prakruti',
and in our 'gyanabhyasa', mind doesn't go to 'prakruti'.
Rather, it discovers itself to be awareness.
Hence, there is no sleepiness,
something like the conscious space.
Like space doesn't have in and out concept,
in absolute consciousness there is no concept of consciousness versus inert.

✦ ✦ ✦

MEDITATION 95

Attending satsang and listening alone is not 'shravanam'.

'Shravanam' means to ultimately recognize that the self we have finally arrived at, after the possible rejection of the 'panchakoshas', we have come to the self that is independent of the 'panchakoshas'.

This self at this stage is the one referred by the Sankhya and the yoga and here they stop. Because their foundation is there are as many 'purushas' and one 'prakruti'.

But, after having done all the 'yogabhyasa' and only this much conclusion that I am someone other than the 'panchakoshas', is incomplete.

Hence, after having recognized this 'purusha tattva', through 'samprajnat' and 'asamprajnat samadhi', the next step is that the 'panchakoshas' or the 'prakruti' cannot remain independent of the 'purusha'.

'Prakruti', 'maya' or 'shakti' is 'brahmashraya'.

Hence, from the point of the fire, the burning power is an illusion, meaning, it may appear for those who are other than the fire, But, fire itself is not influenced by it. In the same manner, from the absolute 'purusha' point of view, 'prakruti' creating the duality, and the effect of 'prakruti', both of them are illusions worthy of discarding. Then, what remains is, there is but one 'purusha'. 'Prakruti' begins with movement. Like air begins with movement. Beyond air, in the space, there is no movement. Hence, this is one of the most important practice. That, not only is our 'asana' steady, but breathing must attain and remain, extremely slow and shallow, to ultimately end up in 'kevala kumbhaka'. Hence, the instruction is to remain aware of respiration. Hence, be vigilant, that whether the breathing becomes deep or fast, when we practice this, mind is not created.

✦✦✦

MEDITATION 96

When the mind is unfolded,
either it gets identified with its own modification,
leading to the experience of dream,
or the mind gets identified with the gross body
and the waking world of the gross object begins.
Hence, the whole world is existing in this identification of the mind in the gross body,
or its own modification,
or the mind gets identified with the absence of these two.
Thus, mind has these three stages.
Waking, dream and deep sleep.
We have to work on this mind.
Functional mind knows everything as existing or non-existing.
Thus, we have these three experiences.
Waking, dream and deep sleep.
Non- functional mind experiences 'samadhi'.
Therefore, unless we go beyond the mind,
this world of relativity
will continue to persecute us.
Hence, all spiritual practices transcend the field of experience of mind.
And for that, the instrument is again, the same mind.
How do we solve this riddle?
If we use the mind, relativity begins.
And again, by the use of the same mind,
we have to transcend the mind.
So, let us inquire about it.
There is only one thing we experience,
without the involvement of the mind and thoughts.
and that is our own breathing.
We don't think and breathe and we don't breathe and think

Let Meditation Happen

simultaneously.
    Like the metabolism in the body,
like the old cells in the body are destroyed and new are created.
The body is increasing in age.
All these things happen without the mind thinking about it.
Taking this as a support.
The technique is,
as we are all sitting,
now, be aware of, don't think.
Don't concentrate.
Simply be aware of the breathing as it is happening.
Don't force for 'bhasrika' or 'pranayama'.
I will tell you in four five sentences, and then you practice.
We have to merely be alert that the breathing does not become deep and fast.
If it becomes deep we are heading towards sleep.
If it becomes fast, we are heading towards body identification.
Hence, be aware that the breathing is extremely slow and shallow.
To such an extent,
as if the air movement is within the nostrils. So slow.
And because we are remaining just aware,
we are not thinking.
As a result, mind will disappear and consciousness alone remains.
Feel how the whole body is now included in the mind
and the relative waking world begins.

✦ ✦ ✦

MEDITATION 97

Living as a body, is no spiritual life.
Living through the body is the beginning of a spiritual life.
Living as 'jiva', the soul,
is no spiritual life.
Living through the mind, as consciousness,
is the spiritual life.
Hence, the first step on the spiritual path,
is to practice, not only physically,
but in understanding, how we are someone other than the body.
And come to appreciate and live thereafter.
This must not remain only intellectual understanding,
but also must precipitate as an experience.
Hence, 'yama', 'niyama',
these two spiritual practices,
Yogic pranayama, are meant for self-disciplining.
Don'ts and do's.
'Ahimsa, satya, asteya, brahmacharya, aparigraha'
and the 'niyamas',
'Shauch, santosh, tapas, swadhyaya, ishwara, pranidhan'
When they are sincerely practiced, then it is something like loosening,
or weakening,
the body identification.
And when we are on the seat of meditation,
let us try to experience this.
When the body is placed on the seat of meditation,
we must practice two things.
One, come what may,
we are not going to move the body.
Two, just be aware and never concentrate.
Concentration is a bad practice for the spiritual seeker.

Let Meditation Happen

Concentration takes us away from our own self.
There is no Self concentration,
there is Self awareness.
So, we remain aware of breathing.
Only these two things.
We must be aware of every breath in and out.
Don't forcibly change your breathing.
We are merely aware of breathing.
Now, when this is going on,
take the position like that of space.
Like in a pot,
space is in and out.
We may call it pot space and use it,
but, this pot space is none other than the total space.
In the same manner,
with reference to the body,
we become inside the body.
But, actually, the body is in us, the mind.
Now, take the position,
that you are not inside the body,
but, the body is in you.
Like the pot is in the space.
So, there are three things.
Steady body.
Being aware of breathing.
Being space like.
Now, when you will continue for sometime,
your body will disappear from your knowledge,
and the formless, bodyless, awareness will prevail.
Move your toes and fingers.
Take a deep breath.
See again how we get identified with the body.
The relativity begins!

✦ ✦ ✦

MEDITATION 98

Is there anyone who is experiencing joys and sorrows?

This is not a question. It is an objection. If we can imagine that our reflection which falls in the mirror, does not become enlivened, but, if our reflection falls in water, it becomes enlivened. And also starts talking, interacting. What will be the life for that will be the life for the 'chidabhasa'. When water is shaky, the reflection will also be shaky, and so on. However, when this seeker, the one who thinks he is experiencing good and bad, as a 'chidabhasa', has to again and again, do this inquiry, that this one who thinks 'I' am suffering,

Is he ever existent anywhere?

The one who is born with every thought, and disappears with the conclusion of the thought, when there are hundreds and thousands of thoughts, such a huge population of "chidabhas's" are born. Because of the high frequency of thought eruption, these "chidabhas's", although separate from each other, have no connection whatsoever, yet, gather a status of continuous existence. And then, 'I' the experiencer is born. Hence, all 'sadhana' is come to one single thought.

Discover that this 'chidabhasa' is dependent on reflecting media on one side, called the mind, and the consciousness whose reflection is the 'chidabhasa' on the other side. Hence, it is just an appearance Not real. Thus, consciousness, the 'kutastha chaitanya' alone is the reality behind all experiences, and not the experiencer. Hence, As I told you, don't make a memory of your meditation. The one who did meditation yesterday, died, immediately after meditation class. Don't dig his grave. Thus, we have to understand the importance, of staying in the utter present. Past and future are projections of the mind. Memory creates past. Worries create future. Excitement disturbs the present. Hence, all spiritual practice is to remain in the utter present. Stop the thought formation Don't go to sleep, yet.Remain aware of your breathing. Because we breathe only in the present.

MEDITATION 99

It is because of sheer practice that we develop conviction in our life. Right from childhood we are told that we are Hindus, Muslim, Christian. We are told that we are superior or inferior.

We are told that these are our enemies. And, thus, slowly, slowly, these thoughts become convictions. Much more than that, we live right from childhood as body.

And this conviction goes so deep that there is no other possibility in our life. Similarly, the conviction that worldly objects have the ability to give us happiness. We are incomplete without certain things.

The result is, we depend upon so many things, and these agitations in the mind with reference to worldly objects, they become quiet when we obtain the object to indulge. we develop our own conclusions. That what I thought, that the object is the source of happiness, is true.

I am happy enjoying this object, And as we grow, this conviction, that happiness is somewhere else and I am seeking that, grows.

But, when we understand, that we are the source of happiness, happiness is not pleasure, happiness is not excitement, happiness is not making loud noise, But then, we even change the definition of a happy life. All these wrong notions are required to be corrected, and to begin, we have to recognize that we are the embodied and not the body. For arriving at this experience, we have to learn to be steady, just like a statue. Relax the body totally, Let the breathing be extremely slow and shallow.

And then, just be aware of the extremely shallow breathing,

which happens as, not breathing through nostrils, but, our whole body expands and contracts, because every cell is breathing. Like the car is different from the movement of the car. In the same manner, the expansion and contraction, is that of the conscious existence. It is because of this conscious existence, that life is possible. This conscious existence is the truth.

MEDITATION 100

When we sit for meditation,
the first thing that comes is,
Now what do we do?
This is because we still have those left over hang ups,
that meditation is to be done.
In fact, not doing,
but undoing.
Hence, to go beyond the doing,
is to go beyond the doer.
And to go beyond the doer is to remain aware.
When we simply remain aware,
To begin with our breathing,
we must be careful about a few things,
that nowhere in us,
as in, lower part of the body,
middle part of the body,
upper middle part, chest, below the neck, back or a bone,
nowhere there is any tension.
Nowhere there is any pressure from inside.
The second important thing,
the moment any thought comes,
it means our awareness is lost,
and we are caught up in the memory lane of the mind.
No thought is good or bad.
We have to go beyond the thought.
Hence, the suggestion,
just remain aware of your natural breathing.
After some time, if we are not carried away by thoughts,
the breathing will become extremely slow and shallow
and then experience for your self, what is next.

✦✦✦

Let Meditation Happen

Books and Cds available at :

Sharda Sangeet Vidyalaya
Nada Brahma Mandir
Madhoosudan Kelkar Marg
Bandra East,
Mumbai - 400 009
Ph. +22 - 26591838

Ajay Usha Kant
The Baby Shop
7/1 Ulsoor Road
Bangalore - 560 042
Ph. +80 - 5599503, 5586105

Yoga Vedanta Association Inc.
14, Meridian Parade
Wantirna South
Melbourne
Victoria-3152
61-03-9837 5995 Home.

Happy Folks Of South Africa
P.O. Box 131426,
Benoni, 1511
Republic of South Africa

Postal Address For Correspondence
Sat Bhavana Trust
128, Brij Kutir,
Dr. M.B.Raut Road, First Floor,
Shivaji Park, Mumbai - 400 028, India.
Tel. No: +91-9820366088

Prabhu Mandhana
S-110 Lohadia Towers
Ashok Marg,
C Scheme
Jaipur - 302 001
Ph. +141 - 2376673

Be Happy Inc.
4169, Bludau Dr.,
Bldg 2410, Warrenton,
VA-20187, USA
(M) 001-703-470-9946

Mr. Prakash Modak
102, Parag, 1st Floor,
Near Andheri Sports Complex.
J.P. Road, Andheri (west),
Mumbai - 400 053
Tel. No. 022-26743330

Padam Chand Gupta
Rajlaxmi Commodities Pvt. Ltd
4033 1st Floor, Naya Bazar Delhi- 6
Mobile: 98100-75276
9873- 64300 (Santosh)
Mail: Padamchandgupta@gmail.com